45 College Recommendation Letters
That Made a Difference

Dr. Nancy L. Nolan

1

Electronic and paperback versions published by:

Magnificent Milestones, Inc.
www.ivyleagueadmission.com

ISBN: 9781933819655

Disclaimers:

(1) This book was written as a guide; it does not claim to be the definitive word on the subject of recommendation letters. The opinions expressed are the personal observations of the author based on her own experiences. They are not intended to prejudice any party. Accordingly, the author and publisher do not accept any liability or responsibility for any loss or damage that have been caused, or alleged to have been caused, through the use of information in this book.

(2) Admission to college depends on several factors in addition to a candidate's reference letters (including GPA, SAT scores, extracurricular experiences and essays). The author and publisher cannot guarantee that any applicant will be admitted to any specific school or program if (s)he follows the information in this book.

Dedication

For students everywhere;
may the size of your dreams be exceeded only
by your tenacity to attain them.

Acknowledgements

I am deeply indebted to the students, professors, employers, and admissions officers who have shared their perceptions and frustrations about recommendation letters. This book, which was written on your behalf, would not be nearly as powerful without your generous and insightful input.

I also want to thank my colleagues at www.ivyleagueadmission.com for providing a constant source of support, along with the best editorial help in the business.

Table of Contents

**45 College Recommendation Letters
That Made a Difference**

Chapter 1: How Academic References / Recommendations are Used

For most candidates, few experiences are as stressful as applying for admission to a top tier college, where dozens of students compete for every seat in the class. In an exceptional pool of applicants, even a slight difference in GPA and SAT scores can make the difference between admission and rejection. Ironically, despite their zeal to make a great impression on the admissions committee, most candidates tend to overlook an important aspect of the application: their reference letters.

Although academic achievements are important, they are only a small part of the admissions decision. Increasingly, top schools are placing greater weight on the quality and depth of your recommendations. As admissions officers, it is their responsibility to admit talented, multi-dimensional people with the potential to become effective leaders in their respective fields. To do so, they must evaluate not only your intellectual ability, but other traits that are not reflected by grades and test scores.

As a result, reference letters from credible third-party sources who can objectively evaluate your integrity and character are paramount in the evaluation process. In fact, they often play a key role in whether you are offered a seat in the class.

From our perspective, candidates don't place much emphasis on their letters of reference for two reasons:

1. they don't think they can control their contents
2. they don't know the specific steps they should take to improve their recommendations

This publication offers a viable plan for getting reference letters that convey *exactly* the attributes you want the admissions committee to see.

From our perspective, smart candidates give their reference letters that same level of attention that they give to their application essays. They take the time to find the *right* people to say the *right* things in the *right* level of detail. In a highly competitive applicant pool, the choice between two equally qualified candidates often comes down to the quality and depth of their recommendations. Choosing the wrong people to write your letters can have devastating consequences.

Sadly, most recommendations we see are short, vague and non-persuasive; they do little to convince us that the candidate is special enough to earn our support. Getting great letters requires planning, hard work and initiative, but is well worth the trouble.

What Makes a Great Letter?

A great letter supplements the data you have provided the school about your academic and professional history with independent corroboration of your performance and potential. It also provides critical information about your personality, ethics and integrity that isn't captured anywhere elsewhere in the application. The BEST references are short, specific and insightful. They are written by faculty members and seasoned professionals who know you well enough to share specific examples of your best traits.

Here is what the committee hopes to learn from your reference letters:

a. Your specific qualifications, including the depth of your academic and professional experiences
b. Your unique traits that aren't covered anywhere else in the application
c. Your demonstrated commitment to pursuing a particular major
d. How you compare to other candidates with similar aspirations

From our experience, reference letters are the ONLY reliable indicator of several essential character traits, such as humor, maturity and tenacity. Many candidates write compelling essays to convince the committee that they are kind, compassionate and patient, but it carries FAR more weight if an objective third-party confirms that. A thoughtful, well-written reference letter, which includes specific *examples* of a candidate's strengths, can make or break an application.

How Reference Letters are Used

As a general rule, recommendation letters supplement the primary admissions criteria for most colleges and universities, which are your GPA and SAT scores. In highly competitive programs, the applicant pool can quickly be sorted into three categories:

a. candidates with excellent grades and SAT scores: good chance of admission
b. candidates who are borderline cases: application is competitive, but not outstanding
c. candidates with low grades and disappointing SAT scores: poor chance of admission

Unfortunately, if you fall into category c, even great letters of recommendation may not save you from rejection. Highly competitive schools often screen out weaker applicants by imposing a minimum "cutoff" for GPA and SAT scores. Although a reference letter can "explain" a disappointing score, it usually cannot compensate for it. Top schools will only give so much leeway to candidates who do not present a solid track record of success.

In contrast, reference letters for candidates in category a are usually disaster checks. These applicants have exceptional grades, top test scores and impressive essays. On paper, they are everything a university is looking for. Their reference letters must:

a. validate their success
b. document their character, integrity and work ethic

For candidates in category a (excellent grades and test scores), a bad or mediocre recommendation can be extremely harmful. If your reference letters cast doubt upon the positive picture you have created (or reveal a serious character defect), the committee will be less likely to take a chance on you.

Surprisingly, nearly 70% of the applicant pool falls into category b, or borderline. These candidates have competitive grades and SAT scores, but are otherwise not distinguishable from others with similar "numbers." Their acceptance or rejection often hinges on an exceptional intrinsic quality that captures the committee's interest and makes a positive impression. In some cases, this can be their commitment to family, their dedication to community service or their ability to overcome an obstacle. Reference letters from third parties who can document these activities can make or break their applications.

Chapter 2:   Who Should Write Your References

Before you ask anyone to write a letter for you, carefully review the instructions from each school where you plan to apply. From our experience, every school takes a slightly different approach to the recommendation process. Some accept free-style letters, while others expect the reviewer to complete a rating form that includes a dozen different attributes. Some schools specify who should (and should not) write your letters, while others leave the choice up to you.

Schools also differ in the number of letters they require (and accept), with most requiring at least two (and accepting no more than five). Follow each school's instructions *exactly*, regardless of how much it complicates the process on your end. Remember, this is the school's first chance to evaluate how well you follow instructions; it's not the time to be a rebel.

As a general rule, schools expect to see reference letters from the following people:

1.   Your high school guidance counselor
2.   A high school teacher in your intended area of study
3.   A coach, music, drama, or art teacher, if you plan to specialize in one of these areas
4.   Your research advisor, if you have conducted academic research
5.   Your supervisor, if you are currently employed
6.   A supervisor who has observed your volunteer work
7.   A customer or client, if you have launched your own business

In many cases, the school's requirements will automatically determine who writes your letters. If so, approach each author with the information in this publication to ensure that you get the best recommendations possible. On the other hand, if you have a choice of authors (or the luxury of submitting additional letters), try to pick the people who can best support your candidacy.

From an admissions perspective, a substantive letter of reference has three important features. The author:

a. understands the intellectual demands of the school(s) where you plan to apply
b. knows you well enough to evaluate your qualifications
c. is willing/able to provide enough supporting detail to justify his/her assessment

As a general rule, you should avoid sending letters from friends, school alumni, relatives, clergymen or politicians, UNLESS they have personally supervised your academic or professional work and can comment on the specific attributes that are being evaluated in the admissions process. You'd be surprised how many people fall into this trap, not realizing that it actually hurts their chances. Nearly every year, colleges receive letters from Senators, Governors and famous Hollywood stars in support of candidates they barely know. They are not impressed. The admissions process is serious business, not a popularity contest. The committee members are not so star struck that they will give a seat to someone just because her aunt works for the Governor.

Academic References

Surprisingly, even the best students sometimes have trouble producing exceptional letters of reference. Getting great letters requires a considerable amount of planning, particularly in the following situations:

a.   At large high schools, many classes are taught in large lecture halls that hold hundreds of students. Even if you ace the class, the teacher may not know you well enough on a personal level to make an honest assessment of your suitability for a particular college or major.

b.   Older applicants are at a disadvantage if an extended period of time has elapsed since they received their high school diplomas. Even the best teachers and guidance counselors can forget individual students after an extended period of time.

If you are still in high school, here are a few tips to help you stand out in the crowd:

a.   Get to know your teachers
b.   Sit in the front row and ask questions during class

    c.   Try to take an upper-division class with a teacher you particularly enjoy
    d.   Arrange to do a research project with your favorite teacher during your sophomore or junior year
    e.   If you have already graduated, keep in touch with your favorite teachers via email and holiday cards. Later, when you ask for a letter of reference, they will be up to speed on your post-graduate accomplishments.

Choosing Your Authors

The best reference letters are from credible sources that can reinforce and complement the information on your application. Your authors should:

a.   be successful leaders, researchers or scholars
b.   have worked closely with you in school or in a professional environment
c.   regard you as a talented candidate with incredible potential
d.   have sterling academic and professional reputations

Furthermore, these authors must be willing to state that they:

a.   know you well enough to evaluate your suitability for college
b.   have observed your growth and development over time
c.   believe that you compare favorably to other candidates they have observed

Red Flags Regarding Your Choice of Writers

For what it's worth, here are the most common "red flags" regarding reference letters:

1.   A candidate has excellent grades, but does not submit a letter from a teacher or guidance counselor. Many colleges will call the school to find out why.

2.   An older candidate has several years of work experience, but does not submit a reference letter from his/her current employer. We understand that many candidates cannot risk their jobs by sending a letter from their immediate supervisor. At many firms, once your boss knows that you plan to resign to go back to school, your professional options will be limited. Colleges "get" that. If you cannot provide a letter from your boss without jeopardizing your job, you should submit a letter from a client or peer, rather than a supervisor. If you don't, the committee will wonder what you are trying to hide.

3.   A candidate who refuses to waive his right to see his reference letters. In the business world, reference letters are not cloaked in the same level of secrecy as in academia. In fact, most employers will give a candidate a copy of the recommendation as a matter of professional courtesy. If your authors extend this courtesy to you, that's terrific; you will know upfront what they have told the admissions committee about you. But don't insist upon seeing the letter if the author does not offer to show it to you. As a general rule, the admissions committee will view the letter as more forthcoming if you have waived your right to see it.

Challenges to Getting a Great Reference

Even the best candidates have trouble getting great letters. Here are the most common challenges, which we will address later in this publication:

1. Well-intentioned bosses and faculty members who don't know what to say. A great letter offers a critical analysis of your strengths and weaknesses from someone who knows you well enough to make an impartial assessment. The details must reinforce and complement the information in the rest of your application. In selecting your reference writers, you must make sure that they:

a.   are good writers
b.   know what to say
c.   support you without reservation

Be VERY selective in who you ask.

2. Authors whose native language is not English. The best references discuss subtle nuances of a candidate's personality and skills, which requires a strong proficiency in written English. Authors who are uncomfortable with the language tend to write less, which ultimately hurts the candidate.

3. Faculty references who don't understand the non-academic aspects of the selection process. Top-tier colleges attract candidates from different countries, backgrounds, and disciplines. To gain admission to these schools, applicants must demonstrate skills and strengths that are not taught in their high school courses. From our experience, many faculty references simply say, "Sam's academic record speaks for itself." Unfortunately, this is not helpful for highly competitive programs, where leadership and interpersonal skills are as highly valued as academic success.

4. Harried bosses and faculty members who don't have the time to write the letters for you. Rather than decline, they do a haphazard job, which does not enhance your candidacy.

5. Employers who refuse to offer any information beyond your title, salary and dates of employment. For legal reasons, many companies have taken a hands-off approach regarding recommendations; they either refuse all requests or limit their comments to names, dates and titles. Some firms even insist that all letters sent out on their corporate stationary be approved by a manager in human resources, who may not even know you. When you approach someone about writing a letter, don't automatically assume that (s)he has free reign to use his/her corporate logo however (s)he chooses. Company rules may severely restrict what current employees are allowed to say. Make sure that the person you have selected is free to write the type of detailed, enthusiastic endorsement that you need. If not, ask someone else.

6. Authors who instruct the candidate to write his/her OWN letter, which they agree to sign. This is a candidate's dream, until (s)he sits down to write. Sadly, most applicants lack the experience to assume the perspective and tone of someone in the recommender's position. They also don't really know what the committee expects. After viewing thousands of references, most admissions officers have an excellent feel for authenticity. As a result, letters written by the actual candidates are embarrassingly easy to spot (and they are the kiss of death for the applicant's admission chances).

Fortunately, there are ways to tackle each of these challenges and get the letters you deserve. Read on!

Chapter 3:   Using the Rating Scale as a Guide

In most cases, each college will provide its own evaluation form for your reference writers to complete. Although all forms are somewhat different, the one shown on the next page (and in Appendix 1) is a fairly representative sample, which we will use for discussion purposes in this publication. Before you ask *anyone* to write a letter on your behalf, take a look at the evaluation form that each school expects him/her to complete. Study the list of attributes that the writer must assess.

On our sample form, the attributes easily consolidate into four distinct categories:

1. **Academic Ability**:   intellectual curiosity, scholarship

2. **Motivation**:   reliability, perseverance

3. **Professional Strengths**:   judgment, resourcefulness, communication skills

4. **Personal Strengths**:   emotional stability, self-confidence, compassion, empathy, maturity

Note that only a few categories involve your GPA or academic performance. Even fewer relate to your mastery of any specific subject matter. Instead, the attributes are *intrinsic character traits* that govern your behavior in all aspects of life. The BEST letters will come from people who are willing and able to discuss these traits in detail.

Before you ask someone to write a reference letter, take a few moments to list the ways that you have exemplified the traits on the rating scale. Restrict your observations to achievements and activities that your author *has actually observed*. Next, for each trait that you have selected, provide a specific example. These observations, which we will call your **"Match Points,"** will form the foundation of your reference letter.

Sample List of **Match Points** (for Dr. Martin's letter)

1.   **Scholarship**: completed three of Dr. Martin's math classes with an A grade. Will graduate from Andover Academy with a perfect 4.0 GPA.

2.   **Communication skills**: excellent speaker and writer; member of the Andover debate team, which won third place in the national competition in 2012.

3.   **Empathy**: high emotional intelligence; assumed workload for a fellow debater after a debilitating car accident. Visited the student often during her medical leave and provided a consistent source of emotional support.

4.   **Language Skills**: fluent in English, Spanish and Chinese; frequently translate documents and journal articles for faculty members.

5.   **Motivation**: completed a research project about fraternal twins for my psychology class; received an A grade.

We will discuss this list further in Chapter 4.

Sample Rating Sheet

Factors: For each factor below, please indicate your opinion of this applicant's rating on that factor relative to other candidates you have observed.

Ranking Standards:

1. Exceptional, top 5%
2. Excellent, next 10%
3. Good, next 20%
4. Average, middle 30%
5. Reservation, next 30%
6. Poor, low 5%
7. No basis for judgment

Factors:

_____ **Emotional Stability:**   Exhibits stable moods; performs under pressure

_____ **Interpersonal Relations:**   Rapport with others; cooperation, attitude toward supervisors

_____ **Judgment:**   Ability to analyze problems, common sense; decisiveness

_____ **Resourcefulness:**   Originality; initiative, management of resources and time

_____ **Reliability:**   Dependability; sense of responsibility, promptness; conscientiousness

_____ **Perseverance:**   Stamina; endurance, psychological strength

_____ **Communication skills:**   Clarity in writing and speech

_____ **Self-confidence:** Assuredness; awareness of strengths & weaknesses

_____ **Empathy:**   Consideration; tact; sensitivity to the needs of others

_____ **Maturity:**   Personal development; social awareness, ability to cope with life situations

_____ **Intellectual curiosity:**   Desire to learn and extend beyond expectations

_____ **Scholarship:** Ability to learn, quality of study habits, native intellectual ability

_____ **Motivation:**   Depth of commitment; intensity; sincerity of career choice

Evaluation Summary:

Compared to other applicants you know, please provide an overall evaluation of this candidate:

(   )   Exceptional candidate, top 5%
(   )   Excellent candidate, next 10%
(   )   Good candidate, next 20%
(   )   Average candidate, middle 30%
(   )   Weak candidate, bottom 35%
(   )   No basis for judgment

Universal Traits that Colleges Seek

If possible, have your reference letters validate the following universal strengths, which are essential in all academic programs:

Exceptional language skills. Write and speak clearly and concisely. Responds to questions (and dissenting opinions) with confidence and grace. Excellent listing skills - can pick up subtle distinctions in discussions and debates.

Excellent analytical skills. Can think independently and make decisions that require the use of various types of reasoning. Can distinguish relevant details from extraneous information in a data set or case study. These skills are often honed in science, mathematics, and economics classes, which require the integration of data from multiple (and often conflicting) sources.

Thinks "outside the box." In emergency situations, there are rarely hard-and-fast rules to guide a person's judgment. Successful candidates can tolerate this ambiguity and recognize the exceptions that modify general rules. Colleges want to know whether an applicant is likely to be stimulated (or frustrated) by questions (and scenarios) that have no "correct" answers.

Thrives in a rigorous, interactive environment. Candidates who enjoy rigorous discussions and collaborative projects are more likely to flourish in a competitive academic atmosphere. Additionally, students must be diligent and well-organized to keep pace with the amount of reading and memorization that advanced courses require. A mature attitude and healthy sense of humor are highly prized in the selection process.

Chapter 4:   How to Ask for a Reference Letter

Once you have chosen your potential reference writers, you need to ask them if they are willing to tackle the job. Don't assume that every person you select has the time, energy or inclination to write a great letter of recommendation. Thankfully, by following these tips, you can maximize your chances of getting the *right* people to go to bat for you.

a. **Approach.** Don't simply call or send a form to your writers; always arrange for a personal meeting, if possible, or make a phone call to discuss your request (if the writer is not geographically close). Explain your desire to attend a particular college and your need for a comprehensive letter of reference. Discuss any issues or concerns the person has about your candidacy.

Verify orally that (s)he is willing to write a "strong letter of support," not just an average or lukewarm one. If the person declines, do not push the issue. If you sense any hesitation, graciously withdraw the request. You are better off asking someone else who can recommend you without reservation.

A face-to-face meeting also gives the writer an opportunity to ask clarifying questions. For example, which letters are mailed directly to the school and which letters are returned to the student? Which envelopes must have the author's signature on the seal? When is each letter due? By discussing these requirements with your writers in person, you can ensure that your letters arrive at the right place by the stipulated deadlines.

During your initial conversation, feel free to mention the attributes you would like the letter to highlight; make sure that the person concurs with your own self-assessment. Although it is awkward (and somewhat embarrassing) to discuss your perceived flaws, it is *far* better to identify a non-supportive author now, rather than obtain a bad letter of recommendation.

b. **Documentation.** If the person agrees to write an enthusiastic letter, give him/her the following information:

    i.   A cover letter with the names, addresses and deadlines for every letter you need (Appendix 2)
    ii.   The appropriate forms from each school that (s)he will need to complete
    iii.   A summary of your "Match Points," which explain your fit for the program you have chosen   (Appendix 3)
    iv.   A current copy of your resume
    v.   Your application essays
    vi.   Pre-addressed, stamped envelopes for all letters

These documents will make the writer's job easier because they provide the relevant details for him/her to include in the letter. They will also set you apart from the crowd. In my career, I've written hundreds of recommendation letters for students who were seeking jobs, advanced degrees, scholarships and fellowships. Only a small handful provided this information, which is crucial for writing an effective letter. I am always impressed when a candidate takes the time to organize his/her needs and focus my energy in the right direction. By doing this, (s)he already demonstrates many of the skills that are necessary to succeed.

Increasingly, admissions committees expect writers to support the claims that they make in letters of recommendation. If a teacher says "John is a persuasive speaker," (s)he must provide concrete evidence that John is actually a persuasive speaker. Unfortunately, few faculty members keep copies of student papers, quizzes or descriptions of a student's participation in the classroom. For this reason, you should customize the information on your Match Points for each individual author. Remind each person of your accomplishments in his/her class or department; include specific details. Don't assume that they have the documentation on hand to write a great letter.

A caveat for candidates who are still enrolled in high school; from my experience, many seniors do not have a particularly well-organized resume. For academic references, make sure that your resume includes all of the information the author will need to draft a detailed letter. At the very least, please include:

a.   your overall GPA / honor societies to which you belong / awards you have won
b.   outside activities in which you have participated (and any offices held)
c.   work experience, service activities and volunteer work
d.   a brief description of a term paper, project or other accomplishment you want that person to mention

By providing this information in a concise format, you can help your authors make the best possible case for you.

15

c. **Timing.** Arrange for your reference letters no later than September in your senior year of high school (for candidates who have already graduated, at least *six weeks* before you submit your application). Ideally, ask in the middle, rather than the end, of a semester. Usually, by semester's end, most teachers are overwhelmed with requests for letters and yours will simply be another request in the pack. To increase your odds of receiving a more thorough recommendation, submit your request before the big rush. Tell your reference writers all of the places you are applying at your initial meeting, so they can prepare all of the letters at the same time. Don't blindside them with requests for additional letters later on. From my experience, it's far easier to send out many letters at once than one or two at a time.

d. **Copy of the letter.** Without exception, you should waive the right to see your recommendations. Admissions committees place little stock in letters that the applicant insists upon seeing, because they know that the author is less forthcoming than if the reference was confidential. You may, however, ask the author to send a *copy* of the letter to you for your files. This is not a violation of the rules and gives you some assurance of the quality of your reference.

If a writer does not wish to provide you with a copy of the letter, don't insist upon it. Academic references are still mostly confidential, although the tide is turning very slowly towards full disclosure. This is a startling contrast to the business world, where copying the candidate on a letter of reference is standard practice and a professional courtesy.

e. **Format.** Letters from your teachers and guidance counselors should be professionally typed and printed on the school's stationary. Other letters that you request may not automatically come in this format. If possible, ask your writers to print the documents on professional letterhead with a laser-jet or inkjet printer. For some colleges, the writers are not asked to submit a general letter, but to answer specific questions that are listed on a separate form. If this is the case, you should tailor your list of Match Points to address the specific questions that are asked by each school. (We will discuss this extensively in Chapter 5).

f. **Organization.** Organize the forms, envelopes, program descriptions, and other materials you will give to each reference writer in a logical manner. One simple technique is to paper-clip the form, program description, and the school's envelope together. Then, to make sure they remain together, place them in a large padded envelope; write your name, the writer's name and the date the letters are due on the outside of the padded envelope. Remember that you will have to create a separate padded envelope for each person who is writing a reference letter for you.

When you complete Appendix 2 (your request for reference letters), list the schools in chronological order, with the earliest deadlines first. The chronological list makes it easy for faculty members to complete your letters of recommendation on time.

g. **Follow-up.** Two weeks after a writer agrees to send the reference letter, verify that it has reached its destination. If it hasn't, ask him/her to send a second copy. Then, send a thank-you note to each person who took the time to write a letter on your behalf; it not only shows good manners, but will encourage the writer to continue to offer references for future applicants. A terrific example of a thank-you letter is presented in Appendix 4. Your final step, which is often overlooked by busy applicants, is to notify your authors of the final admissions decision. Use the opportunity to re-thank them for their continual support of your career. It is never too soon to build your professional network.

h. **If Asked to Write Your Own.** In some cases, the people you ask to write your recommendation letters may be too busy to tackle the job. Instead, they will instruct you to write the letter yourself and simply submit it back to them for a signature. Most applicants consider this a dream come true. After all, what could be better than a chance to "toot your own horn" under the guise of being your own boss or teacher?

Sadly, most candidates haven't a clue what an excellent reference letter looks like. To assume the perspective and tone of someone in your recommender's position requires a considerable amount of experience. Most letters written by the actual candidates stand out like a sore thumb: they include far too many details that a real reference letter wouldn't mention and they are identical in tone to the candidate's own writing.

We strongly discourage you from trying to write your own letters. Remember, the admissions committee has viewed thousands of letters and has a good eye for what a real recommendation does – and does NOT – say. There are also moral and ethical considerations with writing your own letters. Colleges do not want to admit sneaky candidates who bend the rules to suit their own whim; they want ethical candidates who are willing to obtain an honest appraisal of their credentials from an objective, well qualified third party. Instead of trying to write your own letters, give the author a copy of your Match Points (Appendix 3), which summarizes your fit for your program of choice. Ask him/her to elaborate on those points to complete the letter. If (s)he refuses, ask someone else, who is willing to take the time to write a reference that genuinely reflects your suitability for the program to which you are applying.

Chapter 5:   How to Write a Persuasive Reference Letter

Assume for a moment that you've just been asked to write your first reference letter. If you are like most people, you were totally flattered by the request. After all, when a candidate asks you to recommend him/her for admission to college, it implies that you are an expert on the subject; you know what it takes to succeed in a highly competitive academic environment. But that doesn't mean that you are in a position to endorse the particular candidate who asked you. Before you agree to write a letter, you must have a frank discussion with the candidate about your ability to fulfill his/her expectations.

A.   Establish honestly and directly whether or not you can write a positive letter on behalf of the applicant. If you only have limited knowledge of the person's talents (or a negative impression of him/her), then you cannot in good conscience provide a positive letter. From our experience, an ambiguous or lukewarm reference can cause as much harm as a negative one. Tell the candidate your concerns upfront. Although the conversation may be awkward, it will enable the applicant to address whatever issues you may have. Alternatively, the candidate may decide to pursue a more enthusiastic person to write a letter on his/her behalf.

Note: From our perspective, the most gracious ways to decline a request are to say that you:

1. do not have enough time to do an effective job
2. are not familiar enough with a candidate's work or background to do him/her justice
3. do not have the credibility to impress the committee at that particular school/program

In all cases, try to suggest someone else who can do a better job on the candidate's behalf. By keeping the emphasis on delivering the best letter possible, you can minimize any hurt feelings.

When deciding whether or not to write a letter, remember that your reputation is at stake. If you work in academia (and write numerous reference letters), admissions officers will eventually become familiar with what you have said about other candidates. If you routinely oversell the applicants (or over-inflate their capabilities), after a few years, no one will believe what you say. The best way to retain your credibility is to be highly selective in whom you choose to support. You will write fewer recommendations, but they will be more meaningful in the selection process.

B.   If you agree to write a letter to support the candidate, you must maintain the integrity of the process by personally writing the letter, rather than simply signing a draft that the candidate has already written. However, soliciting ideas from the candidate regarding the focus and content of the letter is not only acceptable, but recommended.

C. Give the candidate a copy of **a Reference Letter Request Form** (Appendix 5), which summarizes all of the information that you will need to write the letter. At the very least, you should have a copy of the candidate's:

1. Resume
2. Application Essays
3. Match Points (Appendix 3)
4. Written permission for you to send a reference letter on his/her behalf (Appendix 2)
5. A complete list of all schools to which the letter should be sent, along with the deadlines for each (Appendix 2)

D.   Before putting pen to paper, be sure to review your organization's policy regarding letters of recommendation. Since most letters are printed on corporate letterhead, many firms have rigid guidelines in place to protect them from potential lawsuits. The common rule is to write only positive, factual recommendation letters that refrain from any type of derogatory remarks. If you cannot adhere to this requirement, you should decline the candidate's request.

Organizing the Letter

As a general rule, reference letters include four distinct parts:

1.   An **introduction**, which explains who you are, your relationship to the candidate, and why you feel qualified to assess his/her suitability for the program. Explain how long you have known the applicant and in what capacity. State your qualifications for writing the recommendation letter. Why should the reader be interested in your perspective? How many other people of the applicant's caliber have you known; why does the applicant stand out?

17

2. A **discussion of the candidate's strengths** and how they relate to the needs of the program. Discuss the applicant's exceptional qualities and skills, especially those that are required to succeed in his/her intended major. As a first step, review the general categories of skills that we presented in Chapter 3. Include your own observations of the candidate's strengths, along with the list of Match Points that the candidate has provided. These observations will form the foundation of your reference letter.

We recommend that authors organize their discussion of the candidate's strengths in the following manner:

a. First, provide a *general assessment of the applicant's performance* and potential for success, in the context in which you know him/her. If the applicant was your student, mention how well (s)he did in your classes and the particular skills (s)he used to accomplish this. If the candidate is your employee, discuss how well (s)he executes his/her job responsibilities. Highlight the applicant's key accomplishments and strengths.

b. Next, discuss the candidate's *oral and written communication skills*. Highlight any publications or presentations you have observed.

c. Discuss the candidate's *maturity level and interpersonal skills*. Highlight exceptional personal strengths, including how well the candidate gets along with others and his/her level of reliability and responsibility.

d. Finally, discuss any *special skills or strengths* the candidate may possess, such as language fluencies, multicultural expertise or a commitment to volunteer work.

For each characteristic or trait that you mention, give specific examples or anecdotes to support what you say. In reference letters, the power is in the details; generalized praise is not particularly helpful.

3. A **comparison** of the candidate to others who have succeeded in college. Give your judgment of the applicant, his/her qualifications and potential. Why should (s)he be considered over other candidates? Write only complimentary (yet factual) observations.

If asked to discuss a candidate's flaws or weaknesses, choose something that can be presented as an opportunity for growth (we offer several suggestions later in this chapter). The best choices are traits that the candidate has already taken steps to correct, such as a lack of knowledge or training in a particular area. Avoid unflattering or derogatory remarks.

4. A **conclusion**, which summarizes the candidate's outstanding strengths and abilities. Offer a strong ending, but don't overdo it. Excessive praise can be viewed as biased or insincere. Finally, list your contact information if you are willing to respond to follow-up correspondence.

Chapters 7 - 15 provide several persuasive college recommendation letters, which use different approaches to convey the applicants' unique strengths. Use the letters as inspiration for your own original writing.

Writing Guidelines

1. As a rule of thumb, the "correct" length for a reference letter is one or two typewritten pages. You should include enough information to supplement the committee's impression of the candidate, without overwhelming the reader with details that are unrelated to the application.

2. Focus on qualitative information, rather than quantitative. By the time the admissions committee reads your letter, they will have already reviewed the candidate's transcripts and SAT scores. Rather than repeat those details, you should share your "behind the scenes" insight into the candidate's performance and his/her potential to succeed in college. To whatever extent possible, you should give the committee information that they could not acquire any other way.

3. Read the candidate's essays to get an idea of the strengths that (s)he is trying to convey to the committee. Ideally, your letter will *complement* (and build upon) the information the candidate has provided in his/her essays without *duplicating* it.

4. Offer a balanced perspective of the candidate. Admissions committees appreciate letters that offer honest

assessments, including areas for growth; they do not expect perfection.

5.   Do not make any statements that you cannot support with facts and examples. Do not editorialize or speculate. If you give an opinion, explain the incident or circumstances upon which you are basing it. Be able to document all of the information that you release. To avoid a possible claim of defamation, do not comment about the candidate's moral character.

6.   Write with enthusiasm. Use powerful words, such as articulate, effective, intelligent, significant, creative, efficient, cooperative, assertive, dependable, mature and innovative. Avoid bland words such as nice, reasonable, decent, fairly and satisfactory. Although they may seem perfectly fine to you, in admissions circles, they scream "average" or "mediocre."

7.   If there are extenuating circumstances that have affected the candidate's academic or professional progress, you should obtain the candidate's written permission to disclose that information. Colleges value the perspective of someone who knows an applicant well, especially in reference to possible challenges that (s)he has overcome. Nevertheless, these topics (such as homelessness, poverty, divorce, or illness) should NOT be discussed in your letter without the candidate's permission.

8.   Do **not** reveal any information that could be viewed as discriminatory, including the candidate's race, color, religion, national origin, political affiliation, age, disability, sexual orientation, physical appearance, citizenship status or marital status.

9.   If you are an alumnus of the school to which the candidate is applying (or have completed a similar program), feel free to elaborate on the applicant's fit for that particular program. Explain how (s)he will add to the student body and be a good role model.

10.   Type your letter on official letterhead and sign it in ink. A professional presentation will reflect positively on the candidate. Handwritten letters are not only difficult to read, but detract markedly from the writer's credibility. Sadly, admissions committees rarely take the time to read them.

11.   If a candidate asks you to address a letter "to whom it may concern," note that in the body of the letter. Also note that the candidate has agreed to take responsibility for disseminating the letter to the proper person.

12.   If your company has concerns about liability issues regarding reference letters, include the following sentence at the end of your letter:

"This information is provided at the request of [name of applicant], who has asked me to serve as a reference. My comments are confidential and should be treated as such. They reflect my own opinions about the candidate's suitability for college. No other use or inference is intended."

This type of disclaimer explains the purpose of your letter and confirms that it was not written to hurt the applicant's reputation.

13.   Ask the candidate to let you know the committee's decision.

14.   Keep a copy of every letter you send – and document when you sent it. This information will come in handy if, for whatever reason, the letter does not reach its destination (and must be re-sent).

Explaining Weaknesses

For most authors, the trickiest part of writing a reference letter is discussing a candidate's "weaknesses" or "areas of development." Few writers want to document an applicant's faults on record, for both personal and legal reasons. Nevertheless, the BEST recommendations give a balanced perspective of the applicant, including a brief assessment of the areas in which (s)he can improve. If you omit this section, or offer an insincere reply, your letter will lose a portion of its integrity.

From our perspective, the best weaknesses to mention fall into three categories:

1. Areas that the candidate is already working on

Examples:

A poor public speaker who improves his/her skills by joining Toastmasters
Someone with no computer skills who takes a programming class
A candidate who joins a professional association to expand his/her network

2. Areas that will be addressed through the program to which (s)he is applying

Examples:

A candidate with no international experience who applies to a program overseas
A poor typist who takes a class in keyboarding

3. Positive personality traits that need to be tempered

Examples:

A candidate who works 24/7, to the detriment of his/her personal life
A candidate who needs to reign in his/her sense of humor
A candidate who is overly detail oriented, but misses the big picture
A perfectionist who delivers top quality work, but takes forever to do it

Weaknesses that are Deal Breakers.

From our perspective, mentioning the following "weaknesses" will sabotage the candidate's application, and may leave the writer in a legal quagmire. In these situations, you should decline to write a reference on the person's behalf:

a. candidates who have committed immoral, illegal or unethical acts
b. candidates who cannot get along with other people
c. candidates who are incompetent in their current jobs
d. candidates with difficult personalities

No matter how clever you try to be, the committee will "read between the lines" to try to decipher what you AREN'T saying.

Examples:

Sharon marches to her own beat, which few other students hear.
Because she is fiercely independent, Sharon excels at working alone.
Rather than participate in campus events, Sharon prefers to keep to herself.

Translation: Sharon is a misfit who is NOT a team player. She has low leadership potential.

Examples:

In a few years, when he matures, Brad will undoubtedly fulfill his potential.
Regardless of the circumstances, Brad is always the life of the party.
After a slow start, Brad managed to complete his term paper.
Brad's speech, although short on content, was slick and polished.

Translation: Brad is a funny guy who is hopelessly immature. He's not ready for this commitment.

Common Problems in Reference Letters

Here are the most common problems we observe in reference letters.   If at all possible, avoid sending letters that:

1. are typed on plain paper instead of letterhead.

2. do not include the writer's signature and/or contact information.

3. do not include the confidentiality waiver for the letter (sometimes, students forget to give the form to the writer; other times, the writer forgets to return the form to the school).

4. contain unsupported, over-enthusiastic or generic endorsements, instead of offering useful, balanced insights.

5. concentrate on the writer and/or the class, with only a brief reference to the student.

6. disclose personal and controversial information about the applicant that does not enhance his/her candidacy, including personal or political views.

7. contain school-specific or company-specific jargon that is unfamiliar to the admissions committee. If in doubt, show the material to an intelligent person whose formal education is in a different field. If (s)he cannot understand it, the committee probably won't, either. And, sad to say, they won't be impressed by something they can't understand.

Helpful Phrases for Reference Letters

Chapters 7 - 15 provide numerous examples of successful college recommendation letters. We encourage you to use them as inspiration for your own original writing. As you will see, there are several universal statements that are incumbent in all reference letters. If you aren't sure how to get started, or are struggling with writer's block, consider the following phrases as guidelines:

1. Opening Statements

I am writing this letter at the request of Jane Smith, who is an applicant for your fall class.

I am pleased to write this letter of recommendation for Jane Smith.

Please accept this letter as my enthusiastic endorsement of Jane Smith.

My name is Tom James and I am a Manager at Walgreen's. I am delighted to write a letter of reference for Jane Smith to support her application to XXX.

2. Your Qualifications to Evaluate the Candidate

In my 20-year teaching career, I have advised 50 students on independent research projects.

I have personally supervised 10 interns every summer for the last five years as a trainer for Mercy Hospital.

In my career at Bayside High School, I have taught hundreds of students who sought admission to college.

In my 10 years as the CEO of Infotech, I have supervised 50 other programmers with Jane's education and experience.

3. How well you know the Candidate

I know Jane well, because she attended two of my sections every week, although only one was required.

21

Mark reported directly to me for two years prior to his well-deserved promotion to Manager at Bell South.

We enjoyed several after-class discussions about Jane's research, which offered fascinating preliminary results.

I was delighted when Rita asked me to be her advisor for her senior literature project.

4. Candidate's Greatest Strengths

Rachel has the rare blend of analytical and interpersonal skills that a finance career requires.

Rachel is the hardest working and most tenacious student I have ever known.

Rachel was one of the most productive, caring and effective volunteers I have had the pleasure of knowing.

Rachel's greatest talent is fundraising on behalf of cancer research.

5. Assessment Statements

John is an enthusiastic self-starter with an impressive command of technology.

Despite the competing demands on her time, Alexis consistently produced high quality work in a timely fashion.

By using a highly creative approach, Carter quickly re-defined our expectations of a good manager.

In his four years with us, Ben has completed four of my classes and has been one of our most successful students.

6. Evidence to Support a Strength

Jake is the only student who came to all of my office hours to master financial theory. He was one of only two students to receive an A in the course.

Because of Jane's writing skills, I asked her to draft a report for a major policy decision. Based on Jane's sophisticated 20-page analysis of airborne contaminants, Congressman Jones lobbied the State for additional funding.

Jane's technological and quantitative skills are exemplary; the various scheduling, work-flow and asset management software systems that she developed contained complicated algorithms that are beyond the scope of most developers.

7. Rating or Ranking Statements

Jane was in the top 10% of her class.

Zachary has the best analytical skills of any student I have ever taught.

Rachel is in the top 5% of all students I have known, both in academic achievement and practical skills.

As a teacher, I treasure the rare student who has the talent and skill to make a significant contribution to his field. Zane is one of those rare students.

8. Mild Criticism / Presenting a Weakness

John's only fault is his retiring nature. His modesty sometimes hides his remarkable strengths.

Julie's persistence can turn into stubbornness, but her good nature ultimately prevails.

22

With training in finance, Carl will be better prepared to evaluate projects from a business perspective.

The only area of weakness that I ever noted in Jane's performance was her minimal background in statistics. Fortunately, she is now taking a class at the community college to remedy this deficiency.

9. Candidate's Potential for Success

I enthusiastically recommend David to your school. This passionate, well-rounded student will be an extraordinary physician.

With her exceptional leadership, writing and quantitative skills, Sondra will be a credit to whatever college she attends.

George's leadership potential is superb.

I am confident that Joe will be an asset to student life at Harvard.

10. Closing Statements

I am pleased to recommend John for admission to Yale.

Based on Susan's performance, I am confident that she will succeed at a school of Harvard's caliber.

In summary, I am pleased to recommend Jose without reservation.

From my observation, Zachary will undoubtedly succeed at whatever university he chooses.

General Traits to Emphasize

Depending on your relationship with the candidate, the committee will have different expectations of what they expect your letter to say. As a general rule, these are the traits that are most highly prized in the admissions process.

Remember, when you draft your letter, you should restrict your comments to your actual interactions with the candidate – and the achievements *you have actually observed*. Anything that you've "heard" about the candidate from a third party, regardless of how flattering, will be regarded as hearsay if you repeat it in your recommendation letter.

Academic Strengths

Intelligence, Innovative, Scholarship, Insightful, Analytical skills, Creative Reasoning skills, Well-rounded, Curiosity, Class participation, Mastery of specific subject area, Observant

Professional Strengths

Leadership skills, Versatile, Hard-working, Ethical, Motivated, Independent, Tenacious, Well organized, Ambitious, Planning skills, Self-starter, Technical skills (be specific), Creative, Attention to detail, Resourceful, High energy level, Efficient, Communication skills, Good manager, Attentive listener, Writing skills, Perseverance, Presentation skills, Good judgment, Strong interpersonal skills, Negotiation skills

Personal / Interpersonal Strengths

Friendly, Loyal, Optimistic, Sincere, Polite, Modest, Well-mannered, Sense of integrity, Mature, Reliable, Team player, Flexible, Patient, Generous, Kind, Assertive, Empathetic

Chapter 6:   The Letters: A Quick Summary

As we discussed in Chapter 2, the "perfect" person to write your letter is someone who:

- understands the intellectual demands of a highly competitive college or university
- knows you well enough to evaluate your qualifications
- is willing/able to provide enough supporting detail to justify his/her assessment

From our perspective, the following points are worth mentioning:

1. The candidate's intelligence, worth ethic, and command of a particular subject matter. To document these traits, you should mention the specific classes the student took and how (s)he differentiated him/herself from his/her peers.

2. The ability to speak and write in a clear, logical, and persuasive manner. Ideally, you should offer a specific example to support your praise. For example, if a letter claims that a candidate is a good writer, the author must mention a specific paper or assignment that the candidate completed in an extraordinary way. What was the topic? The length? What was terrific about the paper – was it short, concise, well documented, or unusually insightful? Be specific.

3. The ability to get along with a diverse group of people. All students, regardless of their background or major, are expected to demonstrate a strong love of learning and the appropriate level of respect for their fellow students. To document these points, authors should mention the candidate's participation in class, willingness to help others, and attendance at office hours. If appropriate, the author should also document the candidate's ability to work in a team environment. Is (s)he a natural leader? Did (s)he pull his/her weight on any class projects or presentations? If so, offer specific details.

4.   Other notable contributions to campus life, such as:

a. Participation in outside activities related the candidate's intended major

b. Entrepreneurial ventures the candidate has launched

c. Practical experience in the candidate's intended major, through internships, summer work, or paid employment

d. The ability to succeed in the face of adversity. As we discussed in Chapter 5, this can be tricky if the candidate does not want you to reveal the information. Nevertheless, there are situations in which the committee cannot properly assess the candidate's character and motivation unless they know the whole story. From our perspective, the following factors are worth mentioning:

- The candidate earned excellent grades while working full-time to support him/herself.

- The candidate graduated on time, despite suffering a life-threatening illness or injury.

- The candidate has documented learning disabilities, but did not request special accommodations in the classroom (or for the SAT).

- The candidate was a top performer, despite wrestling with serious personal challenges at home (divorce, death, familial illness, language or cultural barriers).

Although these issues are private – and deeply difficult to talk about – the way a candidate deals with them is an indication of his/her maturity and character. If you have the applicant's permission to mention the issue – and you are willing to do so – you can provide the committee with insight into the candidate's life that they could not acquire any other way.

5. In the closing statement: offer a brief summary of the candidate's qualifications and state the strength of your recommendation (enthusiastic, without reservation, etc.). You should also provide your contact information (phone number and email address) in case the committee wants to confirm your letter or acquire additional details. Although it is highly unlikely that someone will contact you, your letter will have an added level of credibility if you indicate that you are receptive to further contact.

24

Finally, print your letter on your official letterhead and sign it as follows:

John Smith, Ph.D.	(Name, Academic Degree)
Department Head – English Teacher	(Formal Title)
Smith High School	(Affiliation)

In the next few chapters, we present several recommendation letters for college applicants who were accepted to top US colleges. For convenience, we have organized them into specific groups:

Chapter 7: Top Scholars
Chapter 8: Student Leaders
Chapter 9: Candidates who are Unusually Mature
Chapter 10: Passionate about Volunteer Work
Chapter 11: Athletes, Artists, and Actors
Chapter 12: Candidates: Candidates with a Multicultural Perspective
Chapter 13: Letters that Document an Obstacle or Adversity
Chapter 14: Candidates who are Targeting a Specific School
Chapter 15: Candidates with Room to Grow

To protect the privacy of the writer and applicant, the names of all people, classes, schools, places, and companies have been changed.

Chapter 7: Top Scholars

The following recommendation letters were written on behalf of students who were top scholars at their respective high schools. To protect the privacy of the writer and applicant, the names of all people, classes, schools, places, and companies have been changed.

From a Department Head

I am the Head of the Biological Sciences Department at Andover Academy, where Sabrina Hayes will graduate with honors next spring. During this time, I have taught three of Sabrina's AP classes – Biology I, II, and Human Anatomy. I am also supervising her current research project for her Honors designation in the Biological Sciences. Based on her performance in the classroom and lab, I recommend Sabrina wholeheartedly for admission to your school.

Throughout her academic career, Sabrina has carried a perfect 4.0 average and has developed an almost encyclopedic grasp of anatomy and physiology. She has also shown an impressive ability to incorporate this information into the studies we conduct in the lab. Sabrina excels at evaluating data, noting trends, and developing new questions for our work. Through her recent coursework at the community college, she has also acquired extensive experience in statistical design and excellent laboratory skills.

Sabrina's honors project is a self-designed study on the effects of reduced fat diets on athletic performance. Our experimental design includes diets that vary in the amount of animal fat, vegetable fat, degree of fat saturation and degree of hydrogenation. We also examined the role of the newly approved synthetic fat substitute, Olestra. Sabrina's job includes food preparation, serving meals, weighing patients, timing their athletic performance on specific tests, and tabulating the results. Based on her early results, Sabrina has concluded that low fat diets (less than 15% of total caloric intake) yield optimal athletic performance.

Sabrina also works as a tutor in the Biological Sciences department, where she helps students with the lecture and laboratory components of our Biology I and II courses. In this role, she conducts individual sessions with students who have academic deficiencies. Sabrina's lecturing style is casual and light; she has an innate ability to explain complex topics in an understandable way. Many students also enjoy her dry sense of humor. As a result, they have consistently rated Sabrina as one of the most effective tutors at Andover Academy.

On a personal level, Sabrina is a pleasant young woman with a huge smile and an impressive history as an athlete. In 2009, she was a member of the Andover Academy women's track and field team, which scored first place in the US National Athletic Competition. Despite her impressive accomplishments, Sabrina is gracious and down-to-earth, a good friend to everyone she meets. She is also an energetic young woman who has encouraged many of her fellow students to embark on personal fitness regimens. I have rarely met anyone more enthusiastic about the topic!

In recent months, Sabrina has expressed a strong interest in pursuing a career in nutritional research. She has a special interest in the role of nutritional therapy in disease prevention and mediation, which will give her a healthy balance of clinical exposure and laboratory research. From my observation, Sabrina has a gift for the human connections that are required in nutritional medicine. She interacts well with people and has a real empathy for those with physical limitations. I see a definite need in medicine for someone with her background and interests.

I strongly recommend Sabrina for your program and think she will make a unique contribution to your class. Please contact me at 555-555-5555 if you would like additional information.

<u>Our Assessment</u>: By citing the candidate's strengths as a scientist, researcher and tutor, this author provided invaluable support to Sabrina's essays on the same topics. The additional details about Sabrina's discipline as an athlete provided further confirmation of her long-term interest in nutrition and exercise. By highlighting Sabrina's interpersonal skills, including her rapport with her students, the author distinguished her from hundreds of other applicants with similar academic achievements.

From an English / Writing Teacher

I am pleased to write this letter of recommendation for Brittany Douglas, who I taught for four years at Adams High School. As part of her graduation requirements, Brittany completed two of my writing classes and impressed me in a number of ways.

Brittany's talent as a writer is exceeded only by her enthusiasm. In my Contemporary Fiction class, she became increasingly excited about the course material as the year progressed. Although she initially avoided the science fiction genre, Brittany's final short story, "Escape from Babylon," was simply brilliant. In addition to creating likeable characters and a suspenseful plot, Brittany displayed a gift for dialogue, along with a subtle flair for black comedy. Without her knowledge, I submitted the story to *Tremors Digest* for publication. They featured it in their August 2009 issue.

I was delighted when Brittany asked me to be her advisor for her senior literature project. Taking a break from fiction, she opted to do a survey piece on the effects of the 9/11 terrorist attacks on inner city children. The paper required extensive research, including several dozen interviews with students and teachers in the heart of New York City. Rather than scale down her project, Brittany worked nights and weekends to ensure its timely completion. Throughout the project, Brittany proved to be a good listener and compassionate interviewer. Her final draft captures both the innocence of the children and their vague awareness of how life had changed since the loss of the World Trade Center.

In the summer of 2011, Brittany demonstrated her strong analytical, critiquing and writing skills in my AP Seminar entitled Early Classics. Among other assignments, she wrote two strong papers about the Bronte sisters and collaborated with three of her classmates on a skillfully written "period novella." On our final day of class, Brittany led a well-prepared and professionally delivered group presentation that showed her deep knowledge of English literature.

Throughout her academic career at Adams High School, Brittany has consistently demonstrated the following skills:

• Successfully plans and completes long-term projects, including comprehensive papers and manuscripts
• Interacts effectively with a wide variety of people, including her teachers, peers, and interview subjects
• Shows initiative, creativity and persistence in difficult situations
• Speaks and writes clearly and persuasively

In summary, I am pleased to recommend Brittany Douglas to you without reservation. If you have any questions regarding her application, please don't hesitate to call me at 555-555-5555.

Our Assessment: This teacher, who was one of Brittany's mentors, provided valuable insight into her achievements as a published author. When considered in conjunction with her other recommendations, which documented her subsequent success in the world of publishing, this letter confirmed that Brittany has always been a woman of character and ambition.

From a Psychology Teacher

Please accept this letter of support for Mr. Zachary Gardner, who is a 2012 graduate of Philips Academy in New Hampshire, where I have taught for more than ten years. Zachary completed four of my AP classes, including General Psychology, General Sociology, Developmental Psychology, and the Psychology of Addictions. He was an exceptional student: intelligent, enthusiastic and assertive. Zachary's perceptive comments, peppered with his wry sense of humor, invariably brought our classroom discussions to a higher level.

In addition to his considerable academic strengths, Zachary is a gifted and prolific researcher. As a junior, he enrolled in my AP Developmental Psychology course, which required students to complete an entire research project (from literature review to final paper) in just one semester. Zachary tackled his project with gusto and completed his paper in time to present his results at the annual American Psychological Research Symposium (APRS) in St. Louis. Without a doubt, Zachary's presentation was one of the best at the conference. He demonstrated remarkable composure, particularly during the question-and-answer session, in which he was besieged with inquiries that went beyond the scope of his work. I was impressed by Zachary's ability to think on his feet under such stressful circumstances.

During his senior year, Zachary completed a follow-up project to address the questions he had been asked at the previous APRS conference. His subsequent presentation at the annual meeting won first place in the student research competition. To my delight, Zachary has already begun to build a professional network at these conferences by chatting with peers from other institutions about their research. His intellectual curiosity is unparalleled for someone his age.

27

As his advisor, I have been most impressed by Zachary's strong sense of moral responsibility. When Philips Academy implemented an Honor Code in 2009, Zachary was one of its strongest supporters. In class, Zachary eloquently explained how the Honor Code would enhance the reputation of all Philips Academy graduates, because it would assure future employers that a candidate's grades were earned honestly. I respected Zachary's willingness to follow his heart and support an unpopular position. I am certain that he will bring the same strong sense of honor and integrity to Yale University.

Zachary's success is attributable to his rare combination of intelligence, motivation, communication skills and personal strengths. He is an extremely well-balanced young man with the ability to form positive relationships with his peers and faculty members. In his leisure time, Zachary served as a volunteer at the local YMCA and helped with a number of community fund-raising projects. As expected, he brought a strong sense of enthusiasm and goodwill to these endeavors.

 From my perspective, Zachary's only weakness was a painful case of shyness, which initially prevented him from participating in many outside activities. Thankfully, in his junior year, Zachary made a concerted effort to conquer his shyness and make new friends. By the time he began his research project, he was comfortable enough in his own skin to give oral presentations in front of a large group of people. In college, I am confident that he will continue to hone this skill.

I recommend Zachary without hesitation, as he is an outstanding young man in every sense of the word. You will enjoy having him as a student.

<u>Our Assessment</u>: This letter provides an extensive, well-documented discussion of Zachary's strengths as a student, researcher and leader. In several places, the author explains how the candidate's skills will be useful in college. From an admissions perspective, the most compelling section of the letter is the paragraph about integrity; Zachary's ability and willingness to stand up for his principles impressed every member of the admissions committee. By taking the time to document these exemplary personal strengths, which the committee would not otherwise have known about, this professor gave Zachary's candidacy a tangible boost.

From a Guidance Counselor

I am delighted to write a letter of recommendation for Morgan Camden, whom I have known for three years. In addition to having a strong intellect, Morgan is also a free thinker with a unique view of life. As his guidance counselor, I marvel at Morgan's enthusiasm for subjects as diverse as history and wood shop. He is a curious and invigorating young man with a passion for everything that life has to offer.

More than any other activity, Morgan thrives on intellectual connection. One time, during lunch, he led an impromptu discussion of Maya Angelou's book, *I Know Why the Caged Bird Sings*. I was amazed not only by Morgan's familiarity with her writing, but the ease in which he discussed the work with those of differing viewpoints. Two students at the table later told me that they learned more about Maya Angelou's writing from that single hour with Morgan than they had in their entire year of Junior English.

At Andover Academy, Morgan has excelled in all of his English and Writing classes. During his sophomore and junior years, he won first prize in the Ohio Statewide Short Story Competition. His submissions, which pondered cerebral themes such as destiny and loneliness, were elegant in their simplicity. At a young age, Morgan has gained impressive insight about human nature. Fortunately, he doesn't take himself too seriously; at all times, Morgan seems completely comfortable with himself and has the ability to laugh at himself when he has made a mistake.

He demonstrated this quality when he helped to organize our school's diversity workshop last fall. As expected, Morgan led several discussion groups with grace and eloquence; when answering questions about different topics, he followed his inner voice, rather than go along with the crowd. Morgan's insight on sensitive issues, such as poverty, racism, sexism, and discrimination, has earned him the respect of faculty and students alike.

Morgan's desire to explore college courses inspired him to champion an initiative for Andover Academy students to get credit for courses that they complete at Cuyahoga Falls Community College. Thanks to Morgan's efforts, it is not unusual for students to graduate from high school with nearly twenty hours of college credits under their belts. Morgan himself was the first student to take advantage of the new policy, which allowed him to complete 24 hours in English and Spanish at the college level. His 4.0 GPA is a testament to his ability to handle such challenging work.

Each year, I have worked with Morgan to create a schedule to best meet his needs. More than any other student, he

28

has insisted on taking the most rigorous courses possible. Although Chemistry is not his strongest area, Morgan insisted on taking it as a sophomore because he wanted the challenge. His willingness to risk his GPA to expand his knowledge base was inspirational to me.

Outside the classroom, Morgan also gives generously of his time and talent by volunteering as a storyteller at our local library. He also volunteers at a local veterinary hospital, where he helps to find homes for abandoned and hard-to-place animals.

In my twenty years as an educator, I have known few students as hard working, well spoken and intellectually curious as Morgan. I am confident that he will excel in your highly competitive academic environment and bring tremendous spirit to the class of 2016. I offer him my highest recommendation.

Our Assessment: The power of this letter is in the details. By taking the time to document Morgan's achievements as a student and leader, the author showed the committee just how special he was. The letter was well perceived.

From a College Professor in Finance

I have known Kristen Stone since 2010 in my position as an Assistant Professor of Finance at the University of Pittsburgh. After evaluating her performance in two of my classes, I am pleased to support her application to the Economics program at Harvard University.

During her senior year of high school, Kristen approached me about the possibility of taking college courses in Microeconomics and Macroeconomics. Although I was initially reluctant to have someone so young in my classes, Kristen convinced me to give her a chance. To my delight, she quickly became one of my top students.

From her first days in Microeconomics, Kristen demonstrated incomparable analytical skills and an ability to think on her feet. The class tends to be particularly challenging because a major portion of the grade is based on class presentations. For each class meeting, students were asked to research a series of investments and to select the one that was most likely to achieve a specific financial goal. On any given day, students were randomly selected to defend their choices in class.

Kristen was an excellent researcher who understood how to apply basic information to specific scenarios. More impressively, she handled difficult (sometimes hostile) questions from her fellow students with grace and confidence. Even when her choice deviated from the "correct" answer, Kristen demonstrated excellent reasoning skills in selecting and defending her choice. She consistently maintained her poise and sense of humor while other students were reduced to tears.

Kristen also demonstrated an insatiable appetite for learning. She attended my review sessions before each exam and asked intelligent, thought-provoking questions. Kristen also sought relevant opportunities to apply her skills in practical situations. Last summer, she worked as the coordinator for the six-week economics internship program at the University of Pittsburgh. In addition to planning many academic and social events, Kristen served as a liaison with the international students who attended the program. Throughout the summer, she was a gracious hostess who helped the students overcome their initial cultural shock. By the end of the six-week course, Kristen had formed several close friendships with students from across the globe.

On a personal level, I find Kristen to be a delightful and extroverted young woman who is sensitive to the needs of others. Despite her aggressive schedule, she always found time to pursue volunteer activities. On one occasion, Kristen participated in the Take Back the Night rally to promote student awareness about sexual crimes. I later discovered that she had singlehandedly raised $1,000 in contributions to support the group's educational program.

I am delighted by Kristen's decision to major in Economics. With her considerable skills in math and logic, she will bring a healthy balance of quantitative and interpersonal strengths to the program. In my 20-yr career as an educator, I have trained thousands of students with high aspirations for a financial career. I would easily rank Kristen Stone in the top 5% of that group. In all endeavors, she demonstrates intelligence, poise and judgment beyond her youth and experience. Her character and tenacity will be an asset to your program.

Our Assessment: This student completed many college credits during her high school years. In this letter, her economics professor provided a detailed account of her diverse accomplishments at such a young age. The committee was particularly impressed by the professor's discussion about her interpersonal strengths and ability to express herself with confidence. The candidate was an excellent fit for the competitive program that accepted her.

From a Teacher

I am writing this letter in support of Cameron Smith's application to Princeton University. I have known Cameron since he entered Andover Academy as freshman in 2009. Since that time, I have come to know him as a student and through various academic and extracurricular activities. I am certain that he will be a strong asset to your program.

Over the past four years, Cameron has demonstrated exceptional academic ability, motivation and interest in psychology. He has a perfect 4.0 grade point average, which is nearly unprecedented in our school. In one of my elective classes in psychology, Cameron was the first student in 18 years to receive an "A+" grade. He consistently showed an exceptional understanding of the material, along with a passion to learn more. With his powerful combination of knowledge, skills and intellectual curiosity, Cameron will go far in whatever field he chooses.

One of Cameron's key strengths is his ability to analyze, integrate and synthesize information from a variety of sources and apply the essence of this information to an important topic. His senior term paper, titled "Noninvasive Methods of Drug Testing in Law Enforcement," is an excellent example of this ability. I have attached a copy of that paper to this letter.

Cameron's paper documents the history of drug testing and explains why current methods are controversial. As part of his research, Cameron interviewed more than 30 law enforcement officials from federal, state and local crime labs and visited five independent testing facilities. After thoroughly presenting different options, he eloquently defended the continual use of the ELISA screening test. Cameron's paper was unquestionably the best in the class; it was meticulously researched, argued and documented. The paper was also written in a clear and precise style.

The project gave Cameron an exceptional opportunity to use his background in computers and statistics. When evaluating and presenting data, he used computer applications software at each stage of the work (bibliographic search, statistical analysis, graphics production, word processing). After presenting his findings at the annual American Psychological Research Symposium, Cameron submitted his manuscript to *Law Enforcement Monthly* for publication. The finished manuscript reflects positively on both Cameron and Andover Academy.

Cameron is an exceptional student who is highly esteemed by his peers and faculty. As a freshman, he tended to avoid self-promotion and let his achievements speak for themselves. Fortunately, over the past three years, Cameron has matured and become more comfortable in group situations. His intelligent thoughts are valued in class discussions, as is his willingness to go the extra mile to help a friend. In all interactions, Cameron is a man of quiet grace and dignity.

As an active and committed member of the National Honor Society (NHS), Cameron has set a new standard for club activities. His leadership abilities have not gone unnoticed. This past year, he was elected as Secretary of the New England region of the NHS, and gave the keynote speech at their national meeting. As always, he impressed the crowd with his intelligence, charm and self-deprecating humor.

As a teacher, I treasure the rare student who has the talent and skill to make a significant contribution to his field. Cameron is one of those rare students. I recommend him without hesitation for admission to Princeton.

<u>Our Assessment</u>: This author was a distinguished teacher at a noted prep school who rarely gave students such rave reviews. As a result, the committee knew that Cameron was truly something special. By documenting his skills as a researcher and leader, the author gave Cameron an edge in a highly competitive applicant pool.

From a Writing Instructor

I am pleased to recommend Meredith Barns for admission to your institution. I have known Meredith for three years as a student in my creative writing classes. During that time, she has proven to be a creative and prolific writer.

In the classroom, Meredith was a joy to work with. She constantly strove to produce the best manuscripts possible. When working in small groups, she was the natural leader and organizer who championed the group's effort and helped others to understand difficult material. Her composition skills were excellent, and, as time progressed, she had four short stories accepted for publication in student magazines. Her future in creative writing is whatever she chooses to make it.

Meredith demonstrated her impressive skills as a researcher while completing her senior class paper, "Women in

British Literature." To complete the paper, Meredith took the initiative to locate and interview several direct descendants of Jane Austen, who provided invaluable insight into the author's motivation and perspective. Elizabeth Reed, the great-granddaughter of Ms. Austen, graciously provided Meredith with Jane's original notes for "Pride and Prejudice," which have never been made available to the public. Meredith's paper included a rich discussion of Ms. Austen's private thoughts on several notable historical events, which are eloquently captured in her writing. After reading Meredith's paper, I had a greater understanding of life in Ms. Austen's time and the challenges she faced as an author. I subsequently re-read "Pride and Prejudice" with an enhanced perspective.

Outside the classroom, Meredith has lent her writing and editing skills to several volunteer organizations, including Planned Parenthood and the New Orleans chapter of Habitat for Humanity. In 2010, Meredith authored a twelve-page brochure for Planned Parenthood that described their services. She also scripted their commercials for local television. As expected, her material was well written, organized and received in the community. I admire her willingness to lend her skills to causes that she finds admirable.

By actively seeking opportunities to write, Meredith already earns a modest living as a published author. She is an inspiration to other students and faculty members who "can't find the time" to pursue their own projects. On several occasions, Meredith has graciously offered to help her fellow students with their manuscripts. In our 2011 summer creative writing conference, she demonstrated excellent project management skills by compiling a collection of students' short stories about Hurricane Katrina. Later, two of the stories were accepted for publication in a student magazine.

Overall, Meredith is a conscientious, dedicated and exemplary young woman. I am certain that she has the ability and drive to accomplish almost anything she sets her mind to. For that reason, I enthusiastically recommend Meredith for admission to your institution, where I am certain that she will flourish in a community of talented and thoughtful students like herself.

Our Assessment: By validating the candidate's talent as a writer and researcher, this author differentiated her from other applicants to a highly competitive writing program. The letter was well perceived.

From a College Professor

I am honored to write a letter of recommendation on behalf of Ms. Elizabeth Ling, who has applied for admission to Harvard University. In 2011, Elizabeth completed my General Psychology course through the continuing education program at New York University. Her exemplary performance in the class, combined with her passion, maturity, and insight, confirmed her ability to succeed at a school of Harvard's caliber.

Over the course of the term, the students discussed several situations in which patients experienced post traumatic stress disorder (PTSD). They also investigated the most popular treatment modalities, including drug therapy, biofeedback, and mental health counseling. Elizabeth excelled in all aspects of the course, including a term paper on the long-term effects of sexual abuse on children. This topic was dear to Elizabeth's heart, because she had endured a similar type of abuse at the hands of a day care worker. In her class presentation, Elizabeth discussed her experience in an honest and expressive manner, including her current work as a peer therapist for other victims of sexual abuse. Elizabeth's wiliness to reveal this information greatly enhanced the class's understanding of PTSD. They also appreciated her courage and strength under such difficult circumstances. In my many years of teaching, I have rarely encountered a more persuasive or perceptive high school student.

At the end of the term, Elizabeth gave a 30-minute presentation on the topic of bravery. Rather than repeat someone else's thoughts on the subject, Elizabeth interviewed several people in New Orleans, who had miraculously re-built their lives after Hurricane Katrina. For her presentation, Elizabeth created a videotape that summarized the many obstacles they faced to rebuild their homes and lives after the flood had receded. For this moving project, which comprised 50% of her course grade, Elizabeth revealed an extraordinary level of compassion, organization and insight. She also gave her classmates food for thought on what it meant to be "brave." As her professor, I am impressed by her willingness to think "outside the box" and make intelligent and well-reasoned decisions. In honor of her work, Elizabeth received the highest mark in the class, which was a well-deserved achievement.

In my 10-year career as an educator, I have worked with thousands of intelligent and talented students. Few have impressed me as positively as Elizabeth Ling. Her maturity, determination, and exemplary work ethic, combined with her delightful personal qualities, have made her an extraordinary student. If given a chance, she will undoubtedly accomplish great feats at Harvard University.

<u>Our Assessment</u>: This professor not only documented Elizabeth's skills as a student and speaker, but as a survivor who used her own experience to help others. As a result, the reader learned what a strong and exceptional woman Elizabeth was – and the many positive traits that she would bring to college life.

Chapter 8: Student Leaders

In addition to their performance in the classroom, many students distinguish themselves by accepting leadership roles in various clubs and organizations. In this chapter, we present several letters that were written on behalf of students who were committed and organized campus leaders. To protect the privacy of the writer and applicant, the names of all people, classes, schools, places, and companies have been changed.

Student Leader

In a world that rewards conformity and sameness, Monica Barnett stands alone. She is a strong and freethinking person who is courageous enough to defend an unpopular stand with intelligence and grace. As a student leader at Andover Academy, Monica is an inspiring role model. I have rarely seen a "wise old soul" in such a young body.

As her guidance counselor, I am impressed by the way that Monica extends herself through school activities. Monica is an artist, an activist and a leader in student government. She has also taken the initiative to establish clubs and organizations on campus to meet the needs of a diverse student body. Thanks to Monica, we now have local chapters of a Women's Studies Club, a Gay-Straight Alliance (GSA), and Amnesty International at Andover Academy. Monica was a founding member of all three groups and continues to serve as the President of the GSA. By generously giving her time and voice to these groups, Monica has provided a forum for students to discuss contemporary issues of relevance to them. She has been a true "unifier" on campus.

Through this work, Monica has become a strong communicator and a gifted public speaker. Last fall, she gave an impassioned speech about AIDS awareness to a packed auditorium of parents and students. Infusing an equal dose of information and humor, Monica discussed a controversial topic with intelligence and ease. She even moderated the resulting debate, which broke down several invisible barriers between the faculty and students. When I see the positive work that the GSA has accomplished in the community, I know that it is a direct result of Monica's tenacity.

Monica also sets a standard of excellence in the classroom. Equally gifted in English and mathematics, Monica can go in any direction that her heart desires. A creative thinker and full-partner in her own education, Monica will undoubtedly pave the road for new thinking in academics as well as the arts. Should she be accepted to your institution, I am confident that Monica will add enormously to your student culture, both inside and outside the classroom. I recommend her without reservation.

Our Assessment: This author, who is a guidance counselor at a large public high school, rarely has the opportunity to get to know his students on an individual basis. His positive impressions of Monica – and his willingness to documents her strengths as a communicator and leader, set her apart from other candidates from the same school.

Student Leader

Veronica Ryan is an intelligent and vivacious student with big dreams and an even bigger heart. On her first day at Andover Academy, she introduced herself to the class as the "future President of the United States." As her teacher and advisor, I am certain that Veronica will achieve her goal!

In her sophomore year, Veronica began to participate in legal proceedings through the Mock Court. By drafting and defending arguments, she became adept at public speaking under stressful circumstances. Unlike many of her peers, who folded under pressure, Veronica knew how to gain a strategic advantage by preparing intelligent rebuttals to her opponent's arguments. By anticipating the merits of her adversary's position, she ultimately enhanced her own. Debating also satisfied Veronica's competitive spirit. Regardless of the topic or position, she was determined to win.

In September of 2009, Veronica was elected as President of the Student Government Association, which lobbied our county seat for increased funding for the school. As Veronica walked to the podium to present her speech, she faced an audience of 150 legislators and taxpayers. Despite the obvious pressure on her, she remained calm, focused and well-organized, which allowed her to present her case with incredible passion. Although the school did not receive everything Veronica asked for, her real "victory" was the positive impression she made on behalf of Andover Academy. For the first time, the public saw what I saw: an extremely talented young woman who is destined to be a leader.

Veronica's lobbying on behalf of our school funding earned her two prestigious awards at the state level: Student

Senator of the Year and Outstanding High School Advocate. Her success in the political arena confirmed her passion for the law and inspired her to complete an internship in the office of State Senator Pam O'Reilly. Through this experience, Veronica gained a bird's-eye view of how legislation is passed in California. She is already making arrangements to complete a second internship next summer.

Additionally, Veronica is a top student and a community advocate for the Boys and Girls Clubs of San Diego, for whom she developed a website. Whenever possible, she also volunteers for the local chapter of Planned Parenthood, which provides free and low-cost health care services to women in need. In my twenty-year career as a teacher, I cannot remember a student as driven, smart and articulate as Veronica Ryan. Please accept my enthusiastic recommendation on her behalf.

Our Assessment: The strength of this letter is that it focuses on a single topic – Veronica's skills as a speaker and advocate. By highlighting those accomplishments, the author validated the material in the candidate's essays and enhanced her application.

Student Leader

Katherine Watson is a dynamo whose soft voice and small stature belie the dedication that she brings to all of her endeavors. More than anything else, Kathy is passionate about protecting the environment. When she returned to Andover Academy for her senior year, she was finally old enough to vote. While researching various candidates, she realized that few of her peers had any idea of where "their" contenders stood on relevant environmental issues. Determined to make a difference, Kathy decided to run a voter registration drive for the upcoming election. The result was better organized than anything I have seen at the national or state level.

During the previous summer, Kathy had worked with an organization that lobbied to protect the indigenous wildlife. Unimpressed by their "strong arm" tactics, she decided to take a less zealous approach at the school by focusing on information, rather than browbeating. Before the election, Kathy researched all of the candidates. Rather than focus on a specific candidate or party, she used a bipartisan approach; Kathy created a spreadsheet that displayed each candidate, his/her party affiliation, and where (s)he stood on key environmental issues based on his/her voting history. Kathy hung the sheets all over the campus, which ensured that the students would have adequate time to "research" their representatives in local, state and national government.

Kathy also set up tables outside the Student Union that provided voter registration forms and information about the environment. This system worked very well. Many students were interested in voting; now, they had concrete information to guide their decisions. By Election Day, Kathy had registered many students who had never voted before. Although her favorite candidate lost, she felt that she had made a difference. More importantly, Kathy championed her passion for the environment in a manner that helped her to build several satisfying friendships with kindred souls on campus. When I remember the 2010 elections, I will remember Kathy, sitting in the Student Union, discussing environmental issues with teachers, students and staff. She gave everyone on campus a valuable lesson in the power of democracy.

As you might expect, Kathy is a high-energy person with an uplifting personality. In addition to her work on the 2010 election, she has also worked as a leadership trainer and has been elected to various positions in student government. Kathy's positive outlook makes her an effective and valued negotiator on issues that are important to our students.

Kathy has also established an extremely strong academic record, which will allow her to excel in a college of Harvard's caliber. I wholeheartedly recommend her for admission to your school, where she will make a positive impact on the campus culture.

Our Assessment: In this letter, the author positions Kathy as a student leader with a deep commitment to the political process. By explaining her work for the 2010 election, she differentiated Kathy from other applicants with similar grades and interests.

Student Government

Eric Sutton is an engaging young man with a keen intellect and a wide range of interests and abilities. He is also a natural leader who has earned the trust of his faculty and peers at Andover Academy.

As the school principal, I have been most impressed by Eric's leadership on the Student Honor Council (SHC). By choice, Andover Academy relies on the Code of Academic Integrity, which imposes an "honor system" among students. We have a zero-tolerance policy for any type of academic dishonesty; all infractions are investigated and resolved by the SHC. Between 2010 and 2012, Eric was the student member on the council, along with five teachers and administrators (including me). We were all quite impressed by his performance.

Eric's role on the SHC was identical to that of the other members; he evaluated evidence from teachers and students on a variety of academic and behavioral offenses. To investigate the matters properly, all council members were thoroughly trained to question respondents, conduct deliberations and draft written opinions about each case. Since the penalties for infractions were severe, including possible expulsion from school, it was imperative that all council members approach each case with an open mind. From day one, Eric took his responsibilities seriously.

In the two years that Eric served on the Student Honor Council, we investigated and resolved 30 infractions, including three cheating scandals. Despite the "heavy' nature of the work, Eric thrived in this highly interactive environment. On one occasion, after a particularly emotional hearing, I asked him why he chose to participate in something so serious. His answer? To make a meaningful contribution to campus life. Previously, Eric had watched from the sidelines as cheating scandals, particularly those involving cell phones and other electronic devices, were slowly eroding the underlying strength of the Code of Academic Integrity. He wanted to be a part of its salvation.

Few students Eric's age possess the maturity and insight to handle that level of responsibility. I applaud his commitment not only to our school, but to his own internal sense of honor, which guides him to the "right" behavior in all aspects of his life. In my many years at Andover Academy, I have rarely met another student with a comparable sense of maturity or integrity. I am proud to recommend him.

Our Assessment: In a few short paragraphs, this letter confirmed that Eric was an honest and committed man of exemplary character. By discussing his work in the Student Honor Council, the author gave his candidacy the boost it needed in a highly competitive applicant pool.

Student Leader

Joseph Taylor is an outstanding student leader in the Andover community. He is also a talented and hard-working student who continually challenges the limits of his potential.

Recently, Joseph spent several hours with his advisor to finish his outline for his Senior Project in his AP Civics class. The resulting plan, to solicit donations from local businesses in support of cancer awareness, is an ambitious and highly personal endeavor for Joseph. After losing his father to prostate cancer in 2007, Joseph discovered the widespread lack of knowledge about this silent killer. Rather than wallow in grief, he opted to take a productive and proactive stance by becoming a public health advocate in the greater Andover community.

As Co-Advisor of our Student Council, Joseph managed to make the project a campus-wide affair. During the first week of November, the school conducted a fundraiser on behalf of the Great American Smoke-out. All proceeds (more than $2,500) were donated to the American Cancer Society. At Christmas, Joseph chaired a committee that collected food supplies for a local AIDS hospice. Without exception, the students who assisted with the drive were impressed by Joseph's commitment to the cause and his compassion for the patients he met.

Beyond his contributions to the Andover community, Joseph is also a member of the Regional Student Advisory Council and the California State Student Advisory Council, which each require a full day each month for meetings. By carefully planning his work, Joseph has balanced these demands with those of his full-time course load and volunteer activities. Additionally, he is taking two Honors classes in Chemistry and Physics at the University of San Diego, which will allow him to complete his undergraduate degree in just three years.

Whatever challenges he faces, Joseph demonstrates a positive attitude, unwavering determination, and genuine compassion for others. I offer him my strongest recommendation for admission to Brown University, which will benefit from his intellectual gifts and flair for leadership.

Our Assessment: Several teachers wrote letters that documented this candidate's impressive performance in the classroom. This one, however, went several steps further – it revealed his leadership skills and commitment to cancer research and fundraising. By focusing on these points, the author differentiated Joseph from other candidates with similar grades and test scores.

Chapter 9:   Candidates who are Unusually Mature

In every high school, there are a select group of students who are more mature and sophisticated than their peers. As a result, they are more focused in the classroom and more likely to assume a leadership role in various clubs and activities. Additionally, these candidates often have a heightened understanding of who they are, what they want, and what is required to get there, which is reflected by the choices they make and the goals they set in all aspects of their lives.

Many times, a recommendation letter from a teacher, guidance counselor, or supervisor who can document this maturity, along with the candidate's commitment and organizational skills, will give the applicant a definite edge in the admissions process. At the very least, the letter will reveal the candidate's focus and versatility, which is highly prized at top colleges.

In this chapter, we present several letters that were written on behalf of students who were unusually mature. To protect the privacy of the writer and applicant, the names of all people, classes, schools, places, and companies have been changed.

Candidate who is Unusually Mature

Wendy Crawford is a well-liked young woman with a strong inner voice and a sure sense of self. She is well-known at Andover Academy for her devotion to animals and the understated way she contributes to those around her.

Wendy's love of animals is legendary. After joining the 4-H Club in the fifth grade, she has spent many years learning the science behind the care and feeding of animals. In addition to her own collection of dogs and cats, Wendy is also a regular volunteer at the Andover Animal Shelter. Two years ago, she rescued a pregnant dog from the "kill room" of the shelter and nurtured her through the whelping of her eight puppies. Wendy later found loving homes for the mother and offspring. She also nursed her family's horse through a difficult illness last year. The work left its mark on Wendy, and also enabled her to carve out her life's mission. She wants a career that will enable her to care for animals.

Our teachers are impressed by the steadfast efforts that Wendy puts into her schoolwork. She is particularly strong in biology, in which she has completed two AP classes. Wendy has also assumed a leadership role on the debate team by delivering impassioned arguments with confidence and poise. Even under stressful circumstances, she keeps a level head and answers questions accurately and thoroughly. As a result, Wendy has gained a reputation as someone who can be relied upon in a crisis.

With her strong organizational skills, Wendy has a high aptitude for research and investigation. Considering her love of animals, a career in veterinary research is not beyond her reach. Over the past two years, Wendy has matured greatly and has developed a strong sense of awareness about the world. She responds well to feedback and diffuses tough situations with humor and humility.

Considering these diverse strengths, Wendy is an excellent fit for your exemplary program in pre-veterinary medicine. It would be hard to find a student who could offer more to your student culture. For these reasons, I offer Wendy Crawford my most sincere and wholehearted recommendation to your program.

Our Assessment: This letter was significant because it was written by the principal of a large public high school who rarely knew individual students well enough to write letters on their behalf. His familiarity with Wendy was a testament to the positive impression that she had made on him – and her demonstrated commitment to a veterinary career.

Candidate who is Unusually Mature

Michael Cicero is a delightful young man with an insatiable sense of adventure. After traveling the world with his father, a diplomat, he is equally comfortable at a cafe in Bangkok and a movie theatre in San Francisco. Thanks to his early exposure to different cultures and experiences, Michael brings a mature perspective to everything he does.

Although Michael once lacked confidence in his math and science classes, he has developed considerable skills in these areas. Nevertheless, he will always be more "at home" with the social sciences and humanities. Michael has a gift for languages and a passion for world literature. Last year, he decided to do an independent project about Albert

Camus as an extension of his interest in psychology. In his final report, Michael made a plausible argument that Camus was clinically depressed, which was unfortunately masked by his proclivity for drugs and alcohol. Afterwards, Michael and I enjoyed a productive conversation about his research and the conclusions he had drawn, which were logical and persuasive.

Michael's teachers see him as a budding intellectual who is willing to go the extra mile to master new ideas. His Spanish teacher, who is a particularly demanding instructor, regards Michael as one of the most consistently focused and attentive members of her class, who gives every assignment his best effort. From her perspective, Michael's commitment to his work is a pleasure to observe, because he is truly engaged in the material. His passion to become fluent in Spanish has inspired Michael's classmates to increase their own expectations in the class.

Michael also has enough confidence to buck the crowd. Few young men would have the guts to be the lone male student in a home economics class, but Michael does. Although he was offered the chance to elect another subject when the gender imbalance came to light, Michael chose to stay. To everyone's surprise, the class was a terrific place for Michael to hone his debating skills. By presenting the "male perspective" on issues such as shopping, budgeting and meal planning, Michael learned how to consider a new perspective, determine its value to him, and integrate it into his life. Characteristically, Michael learned and contributed much to the home economics class.

Michael's ability to think on his feet enabled him to emerge as a leader of the Andover Academy Debate Team, which won third place in the 2010 Tri-State Competition. Because of Michael's enthusiastic participation on the team, he has become a popular and respected student leader.

For these reasons, I am honored to recommend Michael Cicero for admission to your institution. With an education from Harvard, there are no limits to what this talented and dynamic young man will achieve.

Our Assessment: This candidate was an excellent student with a perfect GPA from a rigorous private school. However, this author (the school principal) did not focus on Michael's grades. Instead, he highlighted the unusual maturity he brought to the classroom, debate team, and independent research project. By doing so, the author helped Michael to stand out in a highly competitive applicant pool.

Candidate who is Unusually Mature

When teachers talk about Theresa Walker, they always use the most flattering superlatives; creative, talented, and hard-working. From my perspective as her teacher and mentor, she is an old soul in a teenager's body. Deeply self-aware, Theresa feels that her mission in life is to somehow make everything better for everyone else – and she takes this mission very seriously.

As the first member of her family to go to college, Theresa takes nothing for granted. In fact, until 2009, when her family received a house from Habitat for Humanity, Theresa and her mother lived in a homeless shelter for two years. In 2008, Theresa miraculously survived a bout of pneumonia with little or no medical intervention. To my amazement, this highly motivated young woman never missed a day of school or submitted subpar work, even when her personal life was in shambles. She is, without a doubt, the most inspirational student I have ever known.

Because of her deep sense of appreciation, Theresa never complains about life; when a problem arises, she simply dedicates herself to finding a solution. A conscientious student, Theresa works at all assignments and projects with uncommon diligence. When the subject matter is tough, she works harder until she gets it right. Quitting is never an option.

Theresa's strong values and inner clarity are an inspiration to others. Even those who don't agree with her positions admire the strength she has to stand behind them. Last year, Theresa organized an anti-cell phone campaign at school. She respectfully solicited the advice of our administration, made an impassioned speech to the entire school community, and posted a petition for students to sign. Theresa single-handedly raised our awareness about an issue of great concern to her and made her argument with skill and tact. Normally shy and reticent, Theresa stepped out of her "comfort-zone" because of her powerful sense of justice. I applaud her willingness to take a stand.

Theresa has depth, maturity, cheerfulness and poise, and is able to create warm bonds with others, regardless of their age or background. She is ready for the many challenges that college will present. Theresa has our highest recommendation.

Our Assessment: Once again, the power is in the details. By citing Theresa's ability to survive an illness and homelessness, the author positioned her as a survivor. Then, he revealed her strengths as a speaker and advocate by citing her petition regarding cell phone use on campus. The committee was highly impressed by her maturity and resilience, which they would not have known about any other way.

Candidate who is Unusually Mature

Randy Durbin is a smart and sensitive young man whose strong Christian values have given him a unique perspective of the world. As a student at Andover Academy, he has been a lightning rod for intelligent discussions about the role of faith in our everyday lives. I greatly admire his ability to stand up for his beliefs without offending those who disagree with him.

I first met Randy during his freshman year. A few weeks into his first semester at Andover Academy, the police officers who had attacked Rodney King were acquitted of all charges. To prevent a violent reaction, our principal called an assembly to allow students to voice their feelings. In our integrated enclave of Los Angeles, the riots that followed the verdict left many people frightened and uncertain. Most of our students sat obediently during the assembly and agreed that the riots were unjustified. But Randy disagreed with the police officer's contention that the prosecutor's case was flawed. He raised his hand and asked respectfully: "None of us saw the evidence. How can we possibly condemn the outcome?" No one offered a response.

That high school assembly was the first time that Randy demonstrated his willingness to think for himself, but it was certainly not the last. Unfortunately, not every teacher has welcomed such dialogue. In his literature class, Randy questioned Henry David Thoreau's perception that materialism was inherently corrupt. His teacher, Mr. Kringle, dismissed his query, claiming that Randy wasn't qualified to criticize the author. Like Randy, I was disturbed by my colleague's insistence that students accept Thoreau's view at face value. Mr. Kringle missed a golden opportunity to engage the class in a healthy debate about Randy's argument.

Sadly, Randy is a rare breed in our school. Many times, his questions are ignored or dismissed as argumentative or irrelevant. To me, they are the thoughts of a highly intelligent young man who views the world through a distinctively loving lens. Randy's willingness to speak his mind was enhanced by his summer course in Switzerland, when he completed a class that was taught by an atheist. Although the two men held opposing views on faith, they engaged in stimulating discussions that forced both of them to examine and articulate their views. Randy returned from his trip with more than an appreciation of the Swiss culture and language; he had also benefited from the intelligence and grace of its people. As his teacher and friend, I am saddened that we could not offer him the same level of stimulation at Andover Academy.

In a world where few people are flexible or passionate enough to engage in intelligent discourse, Randy will always seek out the kindred souls who are willing to be his teachers. His goal, as always, is to develop his mind by exposing himself to the broadest possible sources of thoughts and opinions. Randy has much to offer Harvard; you will be lucky to get him.

Our Assessment: In this letter, the author explains the unique and loving way that Randy views the world, which continually inspires him to question the status quo. More importantly, he showed Randy's willingness to do so in an educational environment that did not encourage independent thinking. Randy was a perfect fit for the world class program in philosophy that accepted him.

Candidate who is Unusually Mature

As a teacher, sister, and administrator at St. Mary's Academy, I have known Renee Walker since she was five years old. She has attended our school for twelve years and is also an active member of St. Mary's Church. After watching her grow up before my eyes, I am delighted to write a college recommendation for this smart and delightful young lady.

Renee is the only child of a devout couple who have given her a solid familial and spiritual foundation. Throughout her childhood, they have encouraged Renee in all of her endeavors and sat front and center at every sporting event, spelling bee and musical concert. Renee's parents, in conjunction with our faculty and staff, have instilled in her a sound belief in a loving God, which guides her thoughts and actions. Renee is, in every way, a kind, loving and generous young woman.

Two years ago, Renee questioned her faith when her mother was diagnosed with cancer. Although she understood on an intellectual level that illness can strike anyone, she wrestled with profound thoughts of abandonment. In her mother's greatest hour of need, where was God?

In the following year, Renee and I became quite close as we discussed her conflicting thoughts and feelings. Fortunately, Mrs. Walker's cancer responded to treatment and she is expected to make a full recovery. And, over time, Renee made peace with the many unexplained challenges that we all face. Although she did not find all of the answers she was seeking, Renee has emerged from this tragedy with a strong faith in God and a renewed certainty that He has a plan for her life.

A positive outcome of Mrs. Walker's illness has been Renee's advocacy work on behalf of the FDA-approval of growth hormones for the treatment of cancer. Few of our students have the power and the passion to champion the cause quite the way that Renee does. In the past year, she has given speeches, written to Congress, and held seminars to raise awareness about this issue, which could potentially save thousands of lives. I commend her efforts to promote such an important cause.

Part of Renee's maturation has been making peace with whatever God's plan for her might be. A positive outcome of her recent tragedy is her acknowledgement that she would like to pursue a career in medicine. An excellent student with a strong intellect and a pure heart, I am certain that Renee will succeed in such a demanding field. Her strength and courage during a difficult time remain a source of inspiration to me. When you meet Renee, I am sure you will agree.

Our Assessment: This letter was written by a school administrator who rarely endorses students in such a personal or enthusiastic way. By sharing Renee's spiritual doubts during her mother's illness, she gave the committee an excellent feel for the girl's depth and sincerity. The material was the perfect complement to her other letters, which focused on her accomplishments in the classroom.

Candidate who is Unusually Mature

Anita Santos has a deep character, a selfless devotion to others, and maturity beyond her years. Academically, she has challenged herself by taking a full load of math, science and Spanish classes throughout her years at Andover Academy. She is also a devout Christian who has assumed a leadership position in our school. For these reasons, I am proud to recommend her for admission to Notre Dame University.

In her freshman year, Anita took the initiative to establish a youth group for teenagers at St. Luke's Church. To fill the need for organized activities, she single-handedly raised money to get the group going. In addition to their social functions, the group also supports several community service activities, such as a food drive, a soup kitchen, and a dress-for-success workshop for disadvantaged women. Anita is a vibrant contributor to all of these endeavors, which allows her to make a tangible difference in her community.

Each summer, Anita spends one month in Costa Rica as a missionary for St. Luke's. During this time, she works on whatever project they give her, from building a church to teaching English classes to a group of abandoned orphans. Although draining, the work seems to energize Anita, who feels a responsibility to give back. She was adopted from the same orphanage as a toddler and feels a special bond with the children and sisters who live there.

A devout Christian, Anita maintains the highest personal and moral standards. In everything she does, she puts the feelings of others first. One time, she struggled to organize a day trip for a group of troubled children. All day long, the welfare of the kids was Anita's top priority. Were the girls having fun? Did they have enough to eat? Would they get home safely? The trip was an unbridled success, thanks to Anita's loving preparations.

In all interactions, Anita is kind, modest, thoughtful and self-disciplined. She will be successful in life because of her unwavering tenacity. When faced with an obstacle, Anita will evaluate the situation clearly and formulate a plan to succeed. Then, she will do whatever is necessary to achieve her goal and add value to the organization she is serving. Ultimately, that is what distinguishes Anita from her peers at Andover. Once she decides to achieve something, she never, ever gives up.

After watching Anita blossom over the past four years, I am confident that she has a bright and promising future. With its spiritual-based curriculum, Notre Dame is a fine place for her to build on the solid foundation that she has established. I am happy to recommend Anita to your institution.

<u>Our Assessment</u>: This letter is a lovely character reference from Anita's guidance counselor, which reveals her accomplishments as a student, leader, and volunteer. By citing these strengths in a clear and honest way, she proved that Anita was a perfect fit for the environment at Notre Dame.

Candidate who is Unusually Mature

A joyful and highly motivated student, Savannah Smith leads by example; her kindness is only exceeded by her determination to excel academically. As the captain of our debate team, Savannah has been deeply committed to skill development and team building. She also provides a much-needed sense of optimism. By building arguments for (and against) different positions, Savannah has become a deep thinker who can evaluate different sides of an issue. She has also learned how to articulate her thoughts in an articulate way, which has dramatically improved her self-confidence. As her teacher – and the advisor to the debate team, I have been amazed by her transformation from shy teenager to mature and insightful woman.

Without a doubt, Savannah's greatest contribution has been her work with Habitat for Humanity. Through tremendous dedication, teamwork, and effort, Savannah and her friends raised enough money to go to a hurricane-stricken area of Florida, where they helped poor families to fix roofs, build steps and frame walls. Regardless of the challenges she faced, including stifling heat and humidity, Savannah jumped in and did whatever was necessary to rebuild a house. In hindsight, this experience was particularly rewarding for Savannah, because it confirmed her commitment of a life of service to others.

As a member of my parish, St. Luke's Church, Savannah has taken the lead in planning a variety of charity fund-raisers and used her creativity to make interesting and fun events for people of many different age and interest groups. She is also a member of our choir, where her angelic voice always manages to hit the high notes. As a peer counselor at St. Luke's, Savannah is a terrific role model for other teens. A great listener and loyal friend, Savannah is the person everyone confides in, because they know that they can trust her implicitly.

If accepted to your institution, I have complete confidence that Savannah Smith will continue to enrich your school culture in every way, just as she has at Andover Academy. She is a true leader, a devoted team-player, and a student who always strives for excellence in all she undertakes. Savannah has my highest recommendation.

<u>Our Assessment</u>: This author has two connections to Savannah; in addition to being her teacher and debate coach, she also attends the same church. As a result, the author could provide the committee with personal insight into Savannah's character that they would not have received any other way. By citing her many accomplishments as a debater, volunteer, and church member, the author differentiated Savannah from other candidates with similar credentials.

Chapter 10: Passionate about Volunteer Work

Some students distinguish themselves in the classroom, while others do so by pursuing their interests in music, art, and athletics. Yet other students fulfill their heartfelt potential – and make their maximum contribution to society – by volunteering for non-profit groups in their communities. For these civic-minded candidates, a recommendation letter from a supervisor or administrator who can personally attest to their devotion to an outside cause is highly perceived in the admissions process. The letter should cite the specific contributions the applicant has made to the organization; it should also emphasize their ability to get along with different types of people. These references, if chosen wisely, can make an application unique and memorable. They can also show how the candidate has used his/her skills in an altruistic manner.

In this chapter, we present several letters that were written on behalf of students who were volunteers in their communities. To protect the privacy of the writer and applicant, the names of all people, classes, schools, places, and companies have been changed.

Environmental Advocate

I have been privileged to know Kevin Scott for nearly three years. I first met Kevin when he visited my office to discuss an ethical concern regarding land development in unincorporated York County. As a State Senator, I often meet with citizens who have a vested interest in the future of our county, yet few have championed a cause as fervently as Kevin.

As a lifelong resident of King's Center, Kevin was a close friend of Cyrus Wright, who owned a 300-acre spread of wetlands, ponds and natural wildlife in historic York County. Before his death, Mr. Wright transferred legal ownership of the property to his children with the understanding that it would "not be developed." Just a few months after Mr. Wright's death, several surveyors and building contractors tried to negotiate a development deal with his children. To Kevin's horror, the non-development clause had never been put into writing, which left the heirs free to dispose of the property as they saw fit. Sadly, it did not appear that their father's wishes were a high priority to the Wright children. When the developers made a large cash offer, the heirs retained an attorney to help them close the deal.

The proposed development, which included a gas station, two strip malls, and a 50-unit apartment building, was both a blessing and a curse to the King's Center community. On one hand, the project would bring much-needed jobs, along with two upscale shopping centers. On the other hand, the ecological ramifications of the proposed development were staggering. Thousands of migrating geese would lose their habitat, which was federally protected by the United States Fish and Wildlife Service. In addition, the proposed environmental changes would threaten the endangered species of bog turtles that are indigenous to our area. Few would likely survive.

When he visited my office, Kevin's concern was protecting the survival of the indigenous wildlife. At my suggestion, he began an aggressive grassroots campaign to fight the development. Through pictures and testimonials, he documented the existence of the turtles to various state and federal organizations. Kevin also displayed the photographs on his web site, which he promoted heavily on local radio stations. At town meetings, Kevin took the initiative to educate the public about the devastating impact the development would have on our ecosystem. With the support of his friends and neighbors, Kevin did everything possible to retain the land's ecological bounty.

Within a matter of weeks, Kevin's work attracted the interest of several regulatory agencies. His preliminary data sparked a subsequent study by the US Fish and Wildlife Service, which protected the area to ensure the survival of the turtles. Due to Kevin's efforts, the development deal was squashed, which left the 300 acres as a source of natural beauty for York County citizens.

Without Kevin's initiative, the battle would have been lost. I applaud his efforts, not just as a concerned citizen, but as an environmentalist and friend. Kevin proved to the community (and himself) that a single person can make a significant difference in the town's future. His success in thwarting the development no doubt inspired his aspirations to pursue a career in government. There is no one better suited for the job.

After college, Kevin can use his passion and skills to infuse the local political system with a much-needed sense of balance in making decisions that affect the community. As a State Senator in a rapidly-growing area, I've watched the community struggle with difficult issues related to land consumption, rising taxes, historical preservation, and the economic incentive of real estate developers. Although one person cannot change the world, an informed advocate can educate the public about the long-term ramifications of community growth. Kevin is just the man to assume that challenge.

: This is a terrific example of a strong recommendation letter that was written by a public figure. In this case, the candidate was an "ordinary" young man who had the passion and confidence to stand up for what he thought was right for his community. This author couldn't comment on Kevin's academic strengths, but he documented his ongoing commitment to public service in a detailed and eloquent way.

Fundraising for Cancer Research

I have known Maria Silvia for three years as a volunteer and friend. Since 2009, we have served as Co-Presidents of the Houston chapter of Gilda's Club, which offers free services and educational programs for cancer patients, survivors, and their families. Maria's talents as a volunteer and fundraiser have greatly enhanced our success at all levels of the organization. I have no doubt that she will be an exceptional public health advocate during her studies at Harvard University.

Maria's greatest talent is fundraising on behalf of cancer research. Like many volunteers, her inspiration comes directly from the heart. As a child, Maria lost both of her parents to cancers that have been strongly linked to specific lifestyle choices. After she worked through her grief, Maria was determined to learn as much as possible about cancer. Afterwards, she opted to become a public health advocate in the Houston community.

Between 2009 and 2012, Maria raised over $40,000 for the Houston chapter of Gilda's Club, which funded an additional wing of our Wyatt Street facility. In addition to our original array of educational and support services, we can now offer free respite services to caregivers who are enrolled in our hospice program. Maria also helped to decorate the newly renovated wing, which created three rooms for out-of-town guests who cannot afford to pay for lodging. Without Maria's aggressive fundraising efforts, these improvements would not have been possible.

In 2011, Maria helped to organize a gala benefit on behalf of Lone Star Oncology Associates, which is a sister organization that offers free and reduced price services to indigent and uninsured patients. She also volunteers at the center, where she draws blood, conducts lab tests and provides emotional support to chemotherapy patients. Thanks to her early experience as a caregiver, Maria understands the challenges that patients endure on their uneasy road to recovery. She is a kind and compassionate friend to all who enter our doors.

Maria is particularly committed to helping patients who lack health insurance. In her role as a public health advocate, she has prepared documents for presentation to Congress about the alarming statistics concerning uninsured women, who are significantly more likely to have non-diagnosed cases of breast, lung, colon, uterine and ovarian cancer. Maria's goal is to encourage a cooperative solution between patients, practitioners, pharmaceutical firms and managed care facilities. With her passion, drive and creativity, she is an excellent person to tackle the job.

Maria is the smartest, kindest, most determined woman I know. I recommend Maria enthusiastically for admission to Harvard.

: This letter documents Maria's impressive ability to survive a tragedy and find meaning in her pain. The committee was deeply moved by her personal story, along with her continual commitment to help other women who suffer from the same disease. Additionally, Maria's work as a community advocate was a great fit for the program in which she eventually enrolled.

Volunteer for a Non-Profit Organization (Transfer Student from a Community College)

For the past three years, Delilah Davis has worked tirelessly for Great Beginnings, which is a non-profit resource center for new mothers in the Milwaukee area. In 2009, Delilah was one of the first high school students to volunteer for us. In subsequent years, she continued to work for our organization during her summer vacations. Despite the competing demands of school and work, Delilah handles her myriad duties with maturity and confidence.

Looking back, I can't imagine that Great Beginnings would have taken off, much less thrived, without Delilah's dedication and commitment. Over the years, she has eagerly accepted every challenge we presented to her, including seemingly impossible ones. At age 15, she solicited donations from local businesses in the community. On her own time, she scouted garage sales and flea markets for inexpensive baby furniture to give to our clients. When our grand opening was delayed for several days because of computer problems, Delilah arranged for a local college student to fix the glitch at zero cost. Needless to say, she quickly became the woman to see for a quick resolution to a million thorny problems.

Delilah's greatest strengths are her sensitivity and commitment to follow through. On more than one occasion, she has listened to our client's problems and taken the initiative to find a solution. Several of our most popular services, including well-baby care and Mommy & Me play dates, are a direct result of Delilah's suggestions. Fortunately, her commitment doesn't stop at the idea stage. Delilah is willing to do whatever is necessary to bring a needed service to the community, even if it means starting from scratch. No job is too big or too hard for her.

For the past two years, Delilah has worked diligently to create a breast cancer awareness program for Great Beginnings. Last August, she helped to negotiate a free mammography program with Milwaukee Community Hospital during National Breast Cancer Awareness Week. She also developed an hour-long educational seminar that she presents at local high schools in the city. With her outgoing personality, Delilah is extremely effective at communicating the risks of the disease and the need for preventive examinations. She easily connects with the audience and spurs them to action.

Delilah's kindness and concern for others will undoubtedly serve her well in the future. I am convinced that she has made such a great contribution to our group because people like her and trust her. They sense her enthusiasm for our cause and want to help us. After she graduates from college, I can easily envision Delilah running a non-profit organization that provides quality health care to people in an underserved area. Based on her performance at Great Beginnings, I can't imagine anyone better suited for the job.

Our Assessment: This letter provides an extensive, well-documented discussion of Delilah's commitment to a local non-profit organization. Thanks to this author, Delilah's independence, maturity and high energy level made a lasting impression on the admissions committee.

Community Service – Peer Counselor

I am pleased to endorse Ellen Everett's application to your program. My first contact with Ellen was during the summer of 2009, when she worked as a counselor at a summer conference for troubled teenagers in Wichita. At the time, Ellen was a sophomore in high school who was filled with enthusiasm for her first "real job." During the course of the week, Ellen immediately established a strong rapport with the kids, which set a positive tone for the entire program. Her ideas for activities were inventive and entertaining; they were also incredibly effective.

Due to the diversity of the participants, there was always the possibility of conflict and confrontation. Many of the students felt intimidated by the large campus atmosphere. While setting limits, Ellen treated all of the children with respect and compassion. The experience had a profound effect on the participants, who responded positively to Ellen's skills and professionalism. Since then, she has been invited to organize similar workshops at several other schools.

Two years ago, when she was a junior in high school, Ellen began to take college level courses at Kansas State University. In the fall of 2010, the university's Counseling Center invited her to participate in their Peer Counseling program, which was a rare honor for someone of Ellen's age and experience. Her skills as a counselor, which were so apparent during her summer in Wichita, were equally impressive at Kansas State. Ellen was an enthusiastic participant who was greatly admired by the K-State students. She is particularly gifted at identifying students' needs, encouraging their contributions, and involving them in the planning process. Her passion for her work was evident, and she became a close friend and colleague during the project.

Ellen has expressed a continued interest in pursuing a career in social services. Based on her superior performance to date, I am confident that she will eventually be a leader in our field. It is exciting to think of the ways in which she might contribute to your program.

I offer Ellen my strongest possible recommendation. She is unquestionably one of the most remarkable young women I have ever met.

Our Assessment: This author is a noted administrator at a social services organization who rarely writes letters of recommendation for high school students. His willingness to endorse Ellen spoke volumes about her performance and character. By citing her strengths in a clear and specific way, the author gave her application a tangible boost.

Camp Counselor

I have known Lori Stone since the summer of 2008. We first met when she became a volunteer counselor at the Englewood Day Camp in Attleboro, Massachusetts, where I am the General Operations Director. Although she had been offered a paid position elsewhere, Lori accepted a volunteer job to serve her community and to gain valuable counseling experience. Industry's loss was definitely our gain!

From the very beginning, Lori proved to be an eager and highly-motivated worker. During her first summer with us, she did a great job keeping the 5- to 8-year-olds busy with a variety of imaginative activities and crafts. Because most of our children are autistic, I wasn't initially sure that they could handle such multi-step projects. Thanks to Lori's unlimited patience, the program was a success. She knew instinctively when the children were confused and she tailored her instructions to suit them. Soon, the children looked forward to their craft sessions as a time to learn new things and feel good about themselves. Once she got started, I didn't have to spend much time supervising Lori. The kids loved her and she had a great first summer.

During the summers of 2008, 2009 and 2010, Lori worked as a paid counselor at the camp – she advanced to the level of Senior Counselor by the end of 2008. I really can't say enough about how well Lori handled her duties throughout those summers. She was definitely my top counselor. Lori has a special knack for communicating with kids in all age groups. They relate to her and hang onto her every word. No doubt, this has a lot to do with Lori's friendly and outgoing demeanor. She was very well liked by the kids, her fellow counselors, and the city managers alike.

Through her position, Lori consistently demonstrated her superior leadership ability. This became particularly apparent last year, when she organized and supervised two off-site field trips to the Six Flags theme park. The trips were a wonderful opportunity for our children to participate in a mainstream activity with other kids their own age. Most of them had never been to a theme park without their parents' presence; few had developed the social skills to handle the stresses of the day. Yet with Lori's coaching, they understood the need to wait in line, stay together as a group, and behave on the bus. Both trips were highly successful, which I attribute mostly to Lori's diligence.

Overall, Lori is a dedicated, hard-working counselor who always puts the needs of the kids before her own. Accordingly, without hesitation, I am pleased to recommend Lori Stone for admission to Harvard. With her amiable personality, love of children, and commitment to helping others, I am certain that she will be a tremendous asset to your program in social services. Please call me at 555-555-5555 if you have any questions.

Our Assessment: By presenting a warm and detailed letter about her volunteer work with children, this writer added a whole new dimension to Lori's candidacy. This letter gave the committee a rare glimpse into the softer side of Lori, which her teachers had never seen. It also sparked a lively discussion at her interview, which led to a positive admissions decision.

Election Volunteer (Transfer Student from a Community College)

I first met Ms. Hannah Reilly in 2008, when she worked on Senator Guy Smith's election campaign in Bangor, Maine. At the time, I was the Deputy Mayor of Bangor and the Chairman of the Maine Chapter of the Republican Party. For most of the year, I campaigned aggressively for Senator Smith's election, which allowed me to work closely with Hannah. For the 2008 election, Hannah's primary responsibilities were conducting research, organizing rallies, and maintaining our computer database. Although she was one of our youngest staff members, she was incredibly passionate and reliable.

Since then, Hannah and I have collaborated on Senator Smith's 2012 re-election campaign, in which he won nearly 70% of the popular vote. During that time, Hannah's responsibilities have expanded dramatically. For the 2012 election, Hannah advanced to the role of volunteer coordinator, which required her to recruit, train, and supervise dozens of volunteers in the Bangor office. Based on her impressive commitment and performance, Hannah was offered a paid position, which required her to coordinate the work of 300 volunteers at 12 different offices in Maine. Her subsequent performance was nothing short of extraordinary.

When I first met Hannah in 2008, I was immediately impressed by her focus and commitment. Although she was still in high school, she was extremely knowledgeable about the political process and deeply invested in the state's future. Senator Smith's liberal policies on health care and immigration resonated strongly with Hannah, which sparked her desire to contribute. During the 2012 campaign, Hannah had just completed her education at Andover Academy, where she led the campus chapter of the Republican Party. As a result, she brought an impressive combination of organizational and interpersonal skills, along with a mature perspective of the New England political scene, to Senator Smith's campaign.

With her excellent organizational skills, Hannah excelled at her myriad responsibilities, including conducting polls, scheduling volunteers, negotiating with vendors, arranging for publicity, and writing speeches, phone scripts, and press releases. For complex tasks, Hannah had a knack for assigning the right people to the right jobs, which made our campaigns more efficient. She also diffused many conflicts between staff members by keeping them focused on their common goal.

From my perspective, Hannah's greatest strength is her power of persuasion. In Senator Smith's campaigns, we faced considerable opposition from constituents who opposed his support of the Iraqi war and his conservative position on gay rights and national health care. To win the support of Independent voters, we needed to communicate the Senator's message clearly, concisely, and persuasively to various audiences. Not surprisingly, we encountered many angry and stubborn people on the campaign trail who rejected our platform and challenged our commitment to our cause. It was Hannah's job to reach those people and convince them that Senator Smith would do an excellent job on their behalf. She did it better than anyone I have ever seen.

Throughout the campaigns, Hannah listened compassionately to our constituents' concerns and addressed them in her speeches and press releases. She also held her own in political discussions with people who were significantly older than she was. By being focused and respectful, Hannah made her points and won the trust of our constituents. In 2012, Senator Smith won the support of more than 75% of Independent voters. He could never have done so without Hannah's aggressive campaigning on his behalf.

Besides her work for our campaigns, Hannah also volunteers at the Bangor Sharing Center, which is a non-profit group that serves women and children who are victims of domestic violence. Whenever possible, Hannah helps them find shelter and file the paperwork for a restraining order. She also negotiates on their behalf with landlords, employers, and utility companies. By fighting for the rights of innocent parties, Hannah has earned the trust of countless people in our community.

With her stellar leadership skills, Hannah has a bright future in the Maine political scene. With this in mind, she has set her sights on a political science/ pre-law major, which will give her a comprehensive background in relevant social, economic, and political issues. I cannot imagine anyone better suited for the program at Harvard.

Our Assessment: The author of this letter is a distinguished leader in the Republican Party, who rarely writes recommendation letters for high school or college students. His willingness to do so in such a detailed and enthusiastic manner was a testament to Hannah's character and skills. By taking the time to discuss her evolution over time, including her work for the Bangor Sharing Center, he gave Hannah's application the boost it needed it a highly competitive applicant pool.

Launched a Non-Profit Organization

I have known Samantha Stanton since 2009, when we played together in the string section of the Spokane Symphony Orchestra. At the time, Samantha was a high school sophomore who was full of enthusiasm and ideas. When she asked for my help in launching a non-profit organization to offer music lessons for inner-city children, I was apprehensive, but intrigued. Samantha's passion for the idea soon won me over. In August of 2009, we officially began to work on Music for Spokane.

Although Samantha didn't have any business experience, she was determined to make the program a success. Her first step was to contact local businesses to raise funds and to pitch the value of our program. Samantha also researched various neighborhoods in Spokane to determine the ones that needed a productive after-school recreational activity for their children. I accompanied Samantha to local schools to try to raise awareness for Music for Spokane. Although she was young, she had a clear voice and an innate persuasiveness. Samantha was so enthusiastic and well-organized that people trusted her. Within a few weeks, she convinced several local music teachers, along with our peers in the Spokane Symphony Orchestra, to become volunteer instructors in the program.

Fundraising was a huge challenge, because we didn't have much money for supplies or expenses. Samantha used her connections with the University of Portland to organize several fundraising events, including a holiday concert that raised $7,000 for Music for Spokane. She also convinced her peers to hold car washes and bake sales, which added to our coffers. Most importantly, Samantha persuaded a national instrument manufacturer to donate more than 200 used flutes, clarinets, and violins that they had taken in as trades. As a seasoned fundraiser, I was impressed by Samantha's persistence, stamina, and creativity. She kept going long after most people would have given up.

Thanks to Samantha's efforts, we started our first set of classes in January of 2010. By the following spring, we had 30 instructors teaching 150+ kids throughout the city. I attribute our success primarily to Samantha's perseverance and my business direction. From the start, everything we needed – time, money, instruments, and lessons - came from the goodness of people's hearts. Samantha did everything possible to satisfy our contributors. Every week, she tracked and reported all of our spending on our public web site. Samantha also made efficient use of our limited resources. Over time, she formed strong relationships with our benefactors and volunteers, who felt a certain sense of loyalty to our cause. By 2011, our reputation in Spokane was so strong that we attracted the attention of a national news outlet, which broadcast a story about us. They also put a donation link on their web site, which attracted $50,000 in donations from caring viewers. This generous sum was enough to pay for a long-term lease on our downtown facility.

In December of 2011, I ended my formal affiliation with Music for Spokane when I moved to New York City for business. By this time, Samantha had outgrown her need for my direction, and easily kept it going in my absence. Indeed, Music for Spokane would not exist without her passion and generosity.

In creating and running Music for Spokane, Samantha has already cultivated many leadership attributes; she is focused, compassionate, and willing to take calculated risks. Samantha is also an excellent manager who can satisfy the needs of different groups of stakeholders. She instinctively understands how to work efficiently with a limited budget.

As the Senior Vice President of Radio City Music Hall, I work with dozens of talented young people. Samantha is an outstanding young woman, clearly in the top 1% of that group. Since we first met in 2009, she has matured into a successful young woman with a passion for public service. I am certain that Samantha will bring the same tenacity and exuberance to Harvard that she brought to Music for Spokane.

Our Assessment: Although he does not identify himself until the final paragraph, this author is a highly-recognized leader in the entertainment industry. His willingness to mentor Samantha and endorse her so positively in a reference letter gave Samantha's essay about the music program enhanced credibility. The committee was also impressed by what this letter DIDN'T say. Rather than try to editorialize on the candidate's academic fit for Harvard, the author restricted his comments to his own interactions with Samantha. As a result, they knew that this letter wasn't forced or coached, which made its contents even more reliable. Fortunately, Samantha also submitted strong letters from several teachers who validated her academic excellence.

Chapter 11: Athletes, Artists, and Actors

In this chapter, we present several letters for candidates who distinguished themselves through their participation in music, art, drama, computers, and sports. To protect the privacy of the writer and applicant, the names of all people, classes, schools, places, and companies have been changed.

From High School Soccer Coach

I am delighted to write a recommendation letter on behalf of Grace Witt, who is one of the most respected students in our graduating class. Although quiet by nature, Grace maintains strong relationships with her teachers and peers that are based on trust, respect, and enthusiasm. She is one of the kindest and most diligent students I know.

For the past four years, I have been privileged to be Grace's gym teacher and soccer coach. Compared to her peers, Grace is an excellent player who is fully committed to the game. She is always the first one to arrive at practice, ready to perfect her kicks and blocks. Further, Grace is an excellent team player who puts the goals of the team before her own. As a result, she has gained a reputation as a selfless person who is willing to support others.

Grace is also a natural leader who has the confidence to think big. A year ago, she led a series of fundraising efforts to subsidize the team's trip to the state championship. Grace also represented Andover on the US Girl's All-Star Soccer Team in 2010, which allowed her to flex her skills among a group of top players from around the country. After speaking to her coaches at the event, who were highly impressed by her performance and character, I am certain that Grace has the maturity, athleticism, and organizational skills that she will need to succeed in college athletics.

Finally, Grace is someone who leads through example. For the past three years, she has volunteered as a soccer coach at a summer camp for disadvantaged children. Additionally, Grace also serves as a peer mentor at Andover, to help new students adapt to our culture and understand our academic expectations. Through these activities, Grace has revealed her impressive ability to encourage and inspire people to achieve their personal best. In honor of her dedication, Grace was recently named as "Most Likely to Succeed" by her high school class.

As her coach, teacher, and mentor, I am thrilled to offer Grace Witt my highest recommendation to your school. She has much to contribute to student life.

Our Assessment: By focusing exclusively on the achievements that she had observed, this coach wrote a focused and persuasive letter that enhanced the candidate's application. After reading it, the committee knew that Grace was not simply a great soccer player, but an effective leader with a big heart.

Figure Skating Coach

It is a pleasure for me to write a reference letter on behalf of Bryan O'Sullivan, who I have coached as a competitive figure skater for the past ten years. During that time, he has consistently demonstrated the self-discipline and determination that are needed to succeed in such a competitive arena. Every day, Bryan spends long hours in training in order to improve his performance. He also serves as a mentor for younger students who are just learning the sport. Without a doubt, Bryan is one of the most gifted and talented skaters that I have had the opportunity to coach. Nevertheless, he is never boastful or arrogant about his skills. Instead, Bryan just works harder in order to achieve his goals.

Last year, while practicing for a regional competition in New York City, Bryan asked me to devise a more challenging routine that would allow him to defeat the reigning champion. For several weeks, we worked tirelessly to create a routine that was original and eye-catching, with all of the required technical elements. Bryan's performance was so impressive that it received national coverage on ESPN. As an added bonus, he not only won the gold medal, but an invitation to judge the event the following year. I am honored to have played a role in such an important accomplishment.

Buoyed by this success, Bryan has recently launched his own coaching business in collaboration with his father. By training other skaters, he has traveled extensively in New England and learned how to speak effectively to different types of people. Accordingly, Bryan has become very mature for his age – he is also devoted to his students and the trust they have placed in him.

As a coach, I have an excellent feel for the level of talent and commitment that are required to succeed as a competitive figure skater. Bryan is one of the few students I have ever met who could potentially compete at the national and international level. Accordingly, in choosing a college, he has focused on programs with a demonstrated commitment in this area. After working closely with him for the past decade – and getting to know him as a person, I am confident that Bryan will rise to the top in this field and be a mentor and role model for others. You will be lucky to have him.

<u>Our Assessment</u>: In this letter, the coach provided Bryan with an enthusiastic endorsement for a program that would allow him to continue training throughout the academic year. By limiting his comments to his own area of expertise, he yielded a strong letter that was focused and persuasive.

From a Softball Coach

When I first met Kelly Green, I was astonished by her size and stamina. At four-foot-nine and 85 pounds, she is smaller than many grade school students. Yet the minute she begins to speak, it is obvious that this young woman is an intelligent, kind and thoughtful person with an infectious sense of humor. As such, Kelly has become a leader and exemplary role model at Andover Academy.

In the classroom, Kelly is a highly disciplined student who holds her own during classroom discussions. She is also a force to be reckoned with on the softball team. She joined the team as a lark during her freshman year, thinking that it would be a good chance to socialize. Soon, however, Kelly discovered that she had a great pitching arm and a true love of the sport. As captain of the team during her junior year, Kelly led the Andover Anteaters to a first place finish in the state finals. She later gave an inspirational interview to a reporter from ESPN. Needless to say, we were all terribly proud of the honor that Kelly and the team brought to our school.

Kelly's career goal of coaching college softball is perfectly suited to her personality and skills. She loves all aspects of the sport and has a knack for building great teams. During Kelly's years at Andover, many people came to our games simply to watch her! Most importantly, Kelly is a serious player who devotes the requisite time and energy to remain at the top of her game. She understands, on a deeply personal level, that success requires more than just talent; it requires devotion, teamwork, and split second timing, with no guarantee of winning. Thankfully, Kelly has repeatedly proven that she is a true competitor who is up to the challenge.

If accepted to your school, Kelly will undoubtedly be a positive force, both on and off the athletic field. She has certainly been a tremendous asset to Andover Academy. As her teacher, coach, and mentor, I am happy to offer Kelly my strongest recommendation. Please call me at xxx-xxx-xxxx if you require additional information.

<u>Our Assessment</u>: This letter is everything it needs to be – short, concise, and on topic. It was well perceived.

Actor / Comedian

Compared to his peers, Tyler Chambers is a chameleon: a serious student, a devoted environmentalist, and a gifted actor who is funnier than a sitcom star. Above all, Tyler is a driven young man who has prioritized his hectic schedule to achieve a healthy balance between work and fun.

Academics do not always come easily for Tyler. Thankfully, he has learned to seek help without worrying about what other students think. Tyler also has the confidence to ask the questions in class that no one else has the courage to ask. As a result, he has gained a reputation for being an aggressive learner who stimulates fruitful class discussions.

After repeated frustration in his math classes, Tyler underwent diagnostic testing to see if a learning disability was hampering him. The results revealed a serious case of "math anxiety," which I have been helping him to conquer. Through the use of novel teaching strategies, Tyler has made great strides in his Algebra class. He not only improved his grade, but learned how to keep his cool during stressful exams and quizzes. Since Tyler and I have implemented these new approaches, he has been a happier and more confident student.

A natural comedian, Tyler is well-known in our community as an entertainer. In addition to starring in several school plays, including the leading role in *Romeo & Juliet*, he also belongs to the Carson City Playhouse. Last year, Tyler made his first appearance at the Trinity Improv in Carson City, where he was so successful that the manager invited him back as a semi-regular performer. Here at Andover Academy, we are sure that Tyler will eventually perform his stand-up routine on the *Tonight Show*. He certainly has the talent and confidence to bring his dream to fruition.

When he is not performing, Tyler champions various environmental initiatives, including a recycling drive on campus, which reduced our non-biodegradable trash by nearly 70%. Tyler also chairs the student Environmental Club, which promotes additional ways to preserve our natural resources. Their current initiative is a proposal that would require the installation of low-flow faucets in all school washrooms. Tyler recently gave an impassioned speech to the school board, including well-researched documentation, on the costs and benefits of the proposal.

As a student, performer, and environmentalist, Tyler thinks deeply about the world around him; he is also passionate about making a difference. I am delighted to offer Tyler my enthusiastic recommendation to your school. Your programs in dramatic arts and environmental science are an ideal match for his interests and goals.

Our Assessment: This letter covers several points in a concise and effective way – Tyler's acting career, environmental projects, and ability to overcome his math anxiety. After reading it, the committee felt like they truly knew the type of person he was and what he would bring to campus life. They also knew that Tyler would be a fun person who would enrich the environment for his fellow students.

Computer Animation

Please accept this letter as my enthusiastic support for Mr. Steven Smith, who is passionate about computer animation. By his junior year, Steve had exhausted the computer classes that were offered at Andover Academy. Consequently, he enrolled in several college-level courses at the University of Wisconsin. At the same time, Steve has taught himself several advanced techniques in computer programming, animation and drawing. For his AP project, he created and produced numerous films using these self-taught animation techniques, which were wildly humorous and imaginative. I have rarely seen another project as successful or ambitious.

At the outset of his adventures in animation, Steve drew all three hundred cells for the movie by hand. Then, he scanned and converted them into electronic files. After adding color, Steve animated them and recorded the voices to the track. Steve found incredible personal satisfaction as the artist, director and producer of the films. By working diligently on something he loves, Steve has found his passion and his life's work.

To share his excitement with others, Steve established an animation club at Andover that has propelled him towards his goal of video game production. His joy is contagious, and he has influenced many other students to follow their own bliss. Steve also designed an interactive web site for the animation club, which helped them to promote their work and recruit new members. Within the first few months, it had 30,000 unique hits from gamers across the country.

In all endeavors, Steve Smith is determined, inquisitive and tenacious. He is also refreshingly down-to-earth and a great human being. If accepted to your school, Steve will bring a clear voice, an unparalleled work ethic, and a strong creative spirit. I am delighted to recommend him for admission to the Massachusetts Institute of Technology.

Our Assessment: This letter, by design, is short and sweet. At a young age, the candidate outgrew the resources at Andover Academy and began to take college courses in computer graphics and animation. In this letter, a teacher from his high school documents Steve's amazing skills in this area, along with his participation in relevant clubs and activities. Combined with the other letters that he submitted, including one from his college professor, the committee had a balanced view of the skills that Steve would bring to the table.

Actor

Martin Curtana is a one-of-a-kind student. To his peers at Andover Academy, he is a vibrant personality who headlines all of the drama club's productions. At the same time, Martin also has a mature and philosophical side that belies his jovial nature.

As his drama teacher, I am deeply impressed by Martin's amazing talents in song, theatre, and dance. Since childhood, he has worked extensively in each discipline in order to develop and polish his skills. As a freshman and sophomore, Martin attended a residential summer program in dramatic arts at Syracuse University, where he developed his acting ability and created life-long friendships with a diverse and talented group of students. From this experience, Martin developed greater independence and confidence as an artist. After his junior year, Martin developed and taught a summer dance program for children at a local arts camp, which allowed him to put his knowledge into practice in a fun and creative way. The camp was so impressed by Martin's skills that they hired him to teach the same program next summer.

Last year, Martin played the starring role in the school's production of "Never Alone." He put enormous effort into the performance by memorizing lines, taking direction and adhering to a strenuous rehearsal schedule. Martin was the perfect choice for the role of Josh, a hopeless romantic with an engaging personality. Nevertheless, a medical emergency nearly derailed his plans. Six weeks before opening night, a rare tumor forced doctors to operate on Martin's right eye. At first, no one knew what effect this would have on his academic or theatrical career, yet Martin refused to accept anything less than a full recovery. With the help of a tutor, he kept up with his coursework and rehearsed with the cast online. Within a matter of weeks, Martin was back on his feet, resuming his full-time course load, and preparing for the role of Josh. He received a standing ovation on opening night for giving the performance of a lifetime.

Martin's perseverance in this situation set a positive example for his peers to emulate; it also revealed his incredible maturity and grace under pressure. As he prepares for college, Martin is beginning to realize that he has many intellectual gifts, and he is enjoying the process of self-discovery. I feel privileged to have witnessed his development into such a talented, sensitive, and creative young man. I am delighted to offer Martin my enthusiastic recommendation for college. Life at Columbia will be infinitely more exciting with him on campus.

Our Assessment: This short but eloquent letter documents Martin's gifts as a performer and incomparable strengths as a person. After reading it, the committee knew that he would make a terrific addition to their drama program.

Chapter 12: Candidates with a Multicultural Background

By design, top tier colleges and universities seek a diverse group of students who will bring different ideas and perspectives to the campus. To assemble such a class, they pay close attention to the personal background of each candidate, including their exposure to other languages and cultures. In this chapter, we present several letters that were written on behalf of candidates who have lived and studied in different countries. To protect the privacy of the writer and applicant, the names of all people, classes, schools, places, and companies have been changed.

Multicultural Background

Soon-Yi Chung is one of the most inspirational young women I have ever known. Since arriving in the United States in 2008, she has worked diligently to learn how to speak and write English. Once she mastered the language, Soon-Yi was determined to become equally proficient in all of her classes. Her efforts, which have yielded a 3.92 GPA and a 2370 cumulative SAT score, have been richly rewarded.

Soon-Yi's drive is so strong because it is generated from within. Through her own efforts, she has developed intellectually, and she is always looking for new ways to challenge herself. Our school philosophy and culture, which emphasize learning through deep engagement in each discipline, has been ideal for her. Soon-Yi's passion for education, particularly foreign languages and cultures, causes others to feel the same way. She is a leader in the classroom who brings out the best in her teachers and peers.

When talking with Soon-Yi, it is easy to feel uplifted, because she is full of enthusiasm. After growing up in China, where women are not afforded the best educational opportunities, Soon-Yi relishes her chance to learn and improve herself, both through her schoolwork and by embarking on her own independent adventures. Soon-Yi's dream is to return to China after she graduates from college and open a university there. During a return visit to China in the summer of 2011, Soon-Yi completed language classes at the University of Beijing and lived with a host family for a month. After observing the blatant discrimination against women, she returned to the US with a renewed passion to achieve her personal and professional goals.

Soon-Yi is also a practical woman who is passionate about protecting the environment. Last, year, she helped our school to develop a recycling policy that kept nearly 50,000 pounds of trash out of a local landfill. This year, she is an Environmental Education Intern at Rocky Mountain National Park, which allows her to share her passion for nature with hundreds of park visitors. I greatly admire the generous and fearless spirit that Soon-Yi brings to this position.

Soon-Yi's decision to pursue a degree in languages is an excellent fit for her talents and goals. Thus far, she already speaks English, Mandarin and Cantonese. This summer, Soon-Yi also plans to take an immersion course in Spanish. If admitted to your school, she will add so much to student life, including her passion for causes as diverse as women's rights and protecting the environment. I will miss Soon-Yi dearly when she graduates; I am delighted to offer her my highest recommendation.

Our Assessment: The strength of this letter is in the details. By documenting the candidate's linguistic accomplishments, international travel experiences, and passion for the environment, the author brought her to life in a memorable way. As a result, Soon-Yi was accepted by her top choice school.

Multicultural Background

As the Principal of Andover Academy, I am proud to recommend Naseem Momin for admission to your school. She is unquestionably one of our brightest and most inspiring students.

By nature, Naseem is a confident and engaging young woman with a deep concern for important social causes. She also has the uncanny ability to recognize the essential nature of a person, issue or principle. After watching *Schindler's List*, Naseem told me that she finally understood the concept of evil, which forced her to see the world differently. At first, she felt paralyzed by the events on the screen and was consumed by grief. Then, Naseem recognized that the hatred and discrimination she observed in the movie also existed in real life – and on the Andover Academy campus. Rather than ignore it or pretend that it did not exist, Naseem decided to become an instrument for change. She organized the Andover Academy Cultural Fair, which allowed our students to share their respective cultures with one another in a lively and respectful way. Without Naseem's thoughtful guidance, it would not have

51

been the successful and uplifting experience that it was.

Naseem's values will sustain her for a lifetime, because they enable her to understand and respect people on a fundamental level. For example, her interest in communications inspired her to take a linguistics course through Harper Community College (HCC). The course was extremely challenging and required Naseem to travel for several hours each week, yet she still managed to obtain a top grade. Afterwards, Naseem used her skills to give an informational seminar about the dual enrollment offerings at HCC. I have rarely attended a more focused, concise, or effective presentation, which inspired several of our students to pursue college courses while still in high school.

Over the years, Naseem has learned to persevere at subjects that do not come easily to her. She has also learned how to listen to others and fully absorb their perspectives before rushing in with her own response. In the past few years, several teachers have praised Naseem's excellent organizational skills, which allow her to balance the demands of her classes with several outside interests. In 2010, Naseem helped to create Andover Academy's first debate team, which went on to win a number of tournaments. In 2011, she recruited a dozen new members to the team while the coach was on maternity leave. By motivating each member individually, Naseem helped them to refine their skills and achieve their personal best.

Equally at home in India and the United States, Naseem is bilingual and bi-cultural. She visits India regularly, which allows her to maintain life-long friendships and connections with her extended family. Naseem is also an avid outdoorswoman who initiates her own hiking expeditions. This spring, she plans to go to Wyoming to participate in a wilderness expedition. In addition, she spent part of last summer teaching archery at a summer camp in Utah.

Naseem wants to make a difference in the world, and I know that she will. In addition to her strong native intelligence, she is blessed with the energy and imagination to accomplish great things. With your renowned programs in the humanities, your institution will provide an excellent environment for Naseem to nurture her academic and social skills. I offer her my highest recommendation.

<u>Our Assessment</u>: By covering numerous points in a relatively short space, this author presented Naseem as a serious and well-rounded candidate who was sensitive, driven, and extremely well-organized. As a result, she was accepted to several top tier programs.

Multicultural Background

I am pleased to recommend Olga Struckova for admission to Harvard University. She is a remarkable young woman whose interests, background, and native abilities continually inspire her to achieve great things.

Olga grew up in Poland and moved to the United States during the eighth grade. This bi-cultural background enables Olga to appreciate diversity and understand the relativity of cultural values. To maintain her fluency, Olga has taken Polish language instruction privately for the past four years. An eager learner, Olga has found many ways to advance her education within our school and beyond its walls. Last summer, she took a European History class at the University of Chicago, which required a lengthy commute from her home. To no one's surprise, Olga attained a top grade and was a vibrant contributor to class discussions.

Grounded and confident, Olga quickly emerged as the leader of the Mundelein Debate Team, which honed her skills as a speaker. In order to fund our many activities, Olga initiated a popular website for other debaters around the world to connect with each other and share information. The site now gets more than 10,000 hits per week and was mentioned in the Jan 2012 issue of *Glamour* magazine.

In her free time, Olga also volunteers at a rest home in her neighborhood that has numerous patients from Poland. Every Sunday, Olga visits them and reads the newspaper out loud in their native language. By extending herself in this manner, Olga stays connected to her cultural heritage. She also brings a source of affection and companionship to people who do not have many visitors. As Olga's teacher, I admire her spirit of kindness and generosity, which is rare in people her age.

To her family's delight, Olga will be the first Struckova to acquire a college education. From my many talks with her, I know that she takes the opportunity quite seriously. In all of her classes, Olga takes the initiative to ask insightful questions, work out answers conceptually, and think beyond the expected. Your institution, which offers a prestigious program in international relations, will provide the academic rigor that Olga needs to further develop her gifts. She is an extremely intelligent young woman with great determination and a deep sense of purpose. Accordingly, I am delighted to offer Olga my wholehearted recommendation.

<u>Our Assessment</u>: This letter, although short, includes enough detail to personalize Olga in the committee's mind and summarize her many achievements. The author particularly highlighted Olga's exceptional character strengths, which differentiated her from other candidates with comparable grades and test scores.

Multicultural Background

I am happy to offer a letter of recommendation on behalf of Ms. Nandika Bard. I have known "Dika" for three years as a guidance counselor and friend. During this time, she has blossomed into a talented photographer with a gift for computer graphics.

In 2010, Dika accepted the position as staff photographer for the school literary magazine that I oversee. Despite her competing priorities, Dika jumped at the chance to show off her skills. At a recent pep rally, she went to a great deal of trouble to get action shots of the team on a stringent deadline. Dika was determined to do whatever was necessary to get great pictures that the players would be proud of. Several of the shots were so impressive that they were included in the Andover Academy yearbook.

Dika is also the chairperson for the local chapter of Eve's Garden, which is a woman's rights organization. As a child in communist Russia, Dika observed several acts of violence against helpless women and children. Now that she is in the US, she is determined to do her part to protect the rights of women on a global basis. Dika's emotional experiences have given her considerable passion for her work, which is an inspiration to other girls on campus.

Dika's accomplishments are particularly impressive, in light of her disadvantaged upbringing. Like many students who come to the US as teenagers, she faced formidable challenges to adapt to a new language and culture. When I first met Dika, she was 14 years old and barely spoke a word of English. Her public school in Bensonhurt had no facilities for ESL, so she learned English on her own by working with an old set of Berlitz language tapes. Obviously, Dika was at a distinct disadvantage during her freshman year of high school, when she competed with native speakers of the language.

Fortunately, Dika refused to give up. After a rocky start, she improved her GPA and found her niche as a photographer and computer expert. Although Dika has excelled in her upper level coursework, she struggled with her English courses and the verbal portion of the SAT. To compensate for this deficiency, she took several elective classes in speech and writing and volunteered as a language tutor for new students from Russia. Eventually, with dedication, Dika learned how to express herself with confidence, both verbally and in writing. Rest assured, Dika's low score on the verbal portion of the SAT does not accurately represent her excellent communication skills. I would not endorse Dika's candidacy if I did not have 100% faith in her abilities.

By far, Dika's greatest strengths are her commitment and motivation. Even in stressful situations, she stays focused on the task at hand and completes her work quickly and effectively. With her engaging personality and commitment to helping others, Dika will undoubtedly be a compelling presence on campus. I recommend her without reservation for your program.

<u>Our Assessment</u>: This author does an excellent job of documenting Nandika's ability to transcend her language and cultural barriers and fulfill her potential as a student and photographer. Her work for Eve's Garden, which she discussed in her Common Application essay, was particularly well perceived.

Chapter 13: Letters that Document an Obstacle or Adversity

Some candidates face formidable obstacles to graduate from high school and apply to college. Due to personal events that are beyond their control, such as illness, language deficiencies, learning disabilities, or cultural barriers, even basic milestones are difficult to achieve. Nevertheless, these extraordinary candidates are top performers in the classroom and work environment because of their insatiable dedication and tenacity. They have a level of focus, maturity, and resilience that sets them apart from the crowd.

Many times, candidates will discuss these obstacles in their application essays, both to share their background with the committee and to document their problems with their classes or the SAT. Unfortunately, in a large applicant pool, it is often difficult to distinguish genuine hardships from ordinary excuses. From our experience, the information will carry *far* more weight if it is confirmed in a recommendation letter from an objective third party who has no vested interest in the admissions decision.

Although these issues are private (and difficult to talk about), the way a candidate deals with them is an indication of his/her character. If you have the applicant's permission to mention the issue – and you are willing to do so – you can provide the committee with insight into the candidate's life that they never could have acquired any other way.

Here are several recommendation letters for candidates who have survived an obstacle or setback. To protect the privacy of the writer and applicant, the names of all people, classes, schools, places, and companies have been changed.

Candidate has Overcome an Obstacle

Richard Sanchez is a bright student with a shy smile and an inquiring nature. He is also an eloquent speaker and writer who can articulate his feelings with an inspiring level of grace. Although Richard's transcript shows an uneven performance, we have witnessed tremendous growth this past year.

In August of 2009, Richard's mother, who was a single parent, was killed in a drunk driving accident. Since then, Richard has been shuffled between the homes of two relatives who are ill-prepared to assume the awesome task of raising a teenage boy. Between 2009 and 2010, Richard wrestled with a profound sense of grief and instability. His struggles to adjust at school were complicated by his erratic home life and lack of familial support. Thankfully, in the fall of 2010, Richard was legally adopted by an elderly couple in Andover. With their nurturance and support, Richard finally started to blossom into the talented and dynamic young man he is today.

In the past two years, the teachers at Andover Academy have been impressed by the great strides that Richard has made. Finally, after overcoming the grief of his mother's death, he is captivated by what the world has to offer. As his guidance counselor, I am thrilled by Richard's commitment to his education, which is fueled by a strong sense of self. Since his adoption, he has conquered his previous problems with procrastination. His work is meticulous, thorough, and always on time.

Richard has also revealed his strong passion to resolve several high-profile human rights issues. Recently, he initiated a group called Students for Justice, which runs a popular website about world political issues. Noting the power of the media to deliver a message, Richard has also worked on our school newspaper and literary magazine, and has helped to get our school-based radio station off the ground. The common theme that runs through all of Richard's activities is his commitment to social justice. By raising awareness for various issues, such as gay rights, health care disparities, and racial discrimination, he is determined to make a difference in the world.

Last summer, Richard took a philosophy course at a local university that inspired him to major in the discipline. It is a perfect subject for a sensitive and thoughtful young man who is trying to find his place in the world. Thoughtful, reflective and mature, Richard has "brought himself up" in many respects. Sadly, he hasn't always had the kind of family support we would wish for our students. Nevertheless, Richard's ability to rise above his early trauma reveals an impressive tenacity that we rarely observe in someone his age.

I recommend Richard with the highest confidence. Please call us if you would like to discuss his candidacy in further detail.

Our Assessment: In his sophomore year, this candidate lost his only parent in a car accident. Then, he endured two years of upheaval before he was finally adopted by a loving family. In this letter, the author documents the obstacles that Richard faced to complete his education. By sharing these details about Richard's life, including his commitment

54

to various causes, he gave the committee considerable insight into his maturity and stamina.

Candidate has Overcome an Obstacle

As the Principal of Andover Academy, I quickly discovered that Meredith Stone was an exceptional young lady. She has an impressive intellect, unparalleled ambition and a dynamic personality. Indeed, she has become a role model for other students on campus. Yet few of her peers or faculty members know of the struggle that Meredith has endured during the last two years.

With little advance warning, her younger brother Cole died of AIDS in 2010. Although Meredith's family had known of his diagnosis, they were emotionally unprepared for his death. At first, Meredith accepted the news stoically and refused to acknowledge her own grief. She decided to keep the news private, rather than share it with the Andover community. As the lone faculty member to know the circumstances of Cole's death, I was both honored and shaken. On one hand, I treasured the trust that Meredith had placed in me to share such personal information. On the other hand, I questioned whether I could provide adequate support to her during such a devastating time.

Amazingly, Meredith completed the spring semester with straight A's and devoted her summer to volunteer work. While most of her friends were at the beach, Meredith worked at a program at her local hospice designed to promote AIDS awareness in the community. In addition to working with patients, Meredith presented more than thirty seminars on AIDS prevention to local schools and clinics in New York City.

Upon her return to school in the fall of 2011, Meredith continued to teach classes and train new participants in the AIDS awareness program. During the past year, she has been a tireless advocate for AIDS prevention in the NYC area. To my delight, by finding a productive outlet for her grief, Meredith has gained an increased appreciation for life's opportunities.

As you peruse Meredith's application, you will see her grades and SAT scores, her numerous awards and accolades, but nothing about her greatest accomplishment of all; she handled profound grief with quiet dignity and uncommon grace. I desperately wanted to relate this episode, because it characterizes what this remarkable young lady is all about.

As she graduates from Andover Academy, I am incredibly sad to see Meredith go, but I am certain that she is destined to achieve great things. She is smart, dedicated and hard-working. She is selfless and outwardly directed. Under volatile circumstances, Meredith keeps her head and finds a workable solution. She is everything that Harvard could possibly desire.

Our Assessment: Rather than recite the candidate's grades and SAT scores, which were presented in other parts of her application, this author documented her work as an advocate for AIDS prevention and education. By telling this story in a detailed and compelling way, the author revealed important aspects of Meredith's character that the reader would not have known about any other way.

Candidate has Overcome an Obstacle

For the past three years, Coral McNulty has volunteered at Orlando Oncology Associates (OOA), which offers free services and educational programs for cancer patients, survivors and their families. As the President of the organization, I am amazed by Coral's talent for fundraising on behalf of cancer research. Like many volunteers, her inspiration is highly personal. At age six, Coral lost her mother to ovarian cancer when she was just 36 years old. In subsequent years, Coral was determined to give back to the organization that had supported her family during their time of need.

Between 2010 and 2012, Coral raised more than $5,000 for OOA, which covered the expenses of a 10-year-old child from Bolivia who had no medical insurance. She also visited the patient throughout his stay at Arnold Palmer Children's Hospital, which revealed Coral's generosity and compassion. Without being asked, Coral raised $800 to purchase a laptop computer for the boy, which allowed him to complete his classes online. She also tutored him in math and science, which are classes that Coral is passionate about. Most importantly, Coral provided the boy with much-needed friendship and support during a terrible time in his life. I have rarely observed a comparable level of empathy and kindness in someone so young.

Recently, Coral faced an emotional setback when her older sister (and primary caregiver) was diagnosed with breast cancer. Amazingly, her sister's illness seemed to enhance Coral's commitment as a volunteer. She has been an amazing source of support to her sister, who is thankfully expected to make a full recovery. In hindsight, the experience solidified Coral's determination to champion women's health issues. With her passion, drive and creativity, she is an excellent person for the job.

From my experience, Coral McNulty is one of the smartest, kindest, and most determined women I know. She will be a wonderful addition to the student body at Harvard.

Our Assessment: By discussing Coral's commitment to the OOA, this author differentiated her from other candidates with similar grades and test scores. This letter was particularly effective for several scholarship competitions in which the selection criteria were based on community service.

Candidate has Overcome an Obstacle

Mary Morris is one of the most inspirational students at Andover Academy. In spite of a long illness last year, which resulted in a diabetic coma, Mary's resiliency and determination have enabled her to keep on top of her studies from home. Her focus and optimism during this difficult time have also given Mary a keen appreciation for her own health. As a result, Mary now views the world through a new lens that offers unlimited possibilities.

Although she has had a bumpy road, Mary has met each of her challenges beautifully. Last year, after she returned to school, Mary decided to complete a project on educational reform in America, which is a particularly hot topic on the Andover campus. She produced an original video, including interviews with several educational reformers, which compared and contrasted the tenets of traditional and progressive schools. From the project, Mary improved her understanding of the learning philosophy at Andover Academy, which uses more "traditional" teaching methods. Mary's video, which was shown at our school assembly, raised a spirited discussion about the future of secondary education. I admire her willingness to undertake a controversial project of this magnitude and complete it in such a timely and effective manner.

Mary has also made great strides in managing her chronic struggle with diabetes, which forced her to develop a strong sense of discipline at a young age. To stay alive, she must test her own blood many times each day and give herself insulin shots. Further, Mary must measure every meal, snack, beverage and bite of food according to strict guidelines. Despite these challenges, Mary has handled her illness with grace and has never used it as an excuse for poor performance. By managing this responsibility, Mary has matured quickly and become an inspiration to our students and staff.

Psychology, which is Mary's chosen field of study, is an excellent match for her inquisitive mind. At an early age, she looked for ways to explore our city and get to know different types of people. In her freshman year, Mary began to volunteer at the Wyatt Soup Kitchen, where she serves meals to disadvantaged residents. Despite the long commute, Mary derives considerable satisfaction from serving others. The experience seems to have given her a deeper understanding of life, in which we all struggle with the same issues and fears.

On a personal basis, Mary is one of the warmest, most compassionate and gentlest students I know. At first, she tried to keep her condition provide; however, Mary eventually realized that she could help others by sharing her experience with other children and their families. For the past year, Mary has been an advocate and peer counselor for the Juvenile Diabetes Association. In fact, she was recently one of five students who were interviewed for a feature article for the *New York Times*. Here at Andover, we are all deeply impressed by Mary's ability to move forward academically despite the complications of her disease.

I am consistently impressed by Mary's fighting spirit, which has made her a role model for her peers. She will be a terrific addition to Harvard.

Our Assessment: This author did more than discuss Mary's struggle with diabetes; he explained the many ways she contributed to campus life, despite the severity of her illness. By including the details about her educational video, volunteer work at the soup kitchen, and experience as a peer counselor, he brought her to life in a way that no one else could. The letter was well perceived.

Loss of Parents

Maria Valenti has a rare combination of intellect, wit, and artistic talent that distinguishes her from other students. Throughout her four years at Andover Academy, she has always taken the most challenging courses, including several AP offerings. This year, Maria has also enrolled in classes in Art History and Computer Animation at San Diego State University, which are an excellent fit for her artistic skills. In 2010, Maria designed and painted a beautiful mural that now adorns our library wall. The work has been profiled in several art magazines and received the first place award in the California Art Competition. We are incredibly proud of the attention that Maria's artistic talent has brought to our school.

Academically, Maria is one of our strongest students. During her junior year, she was inducted into the National Honor Society and named as a California Regional Scholar. In her spare time, she is also a talented equestrian who has assumed a leadership role at the Myers Horse Stables. Since 2009, Maria has been responsible for the care and training of the horses and educating new members of the group. As captain of the club, Maria must engage in formal dialogue with the judges when the scores of her teammates are disputed. In such public events, Maria has displayed her amazing independence and confidence under pressure.

As a computer enthusiast, Maria has also revealed an impressive ability to see opportunities that other people miss. In 2010, she identified the need for an on-site internet cafe at the local coffee house. On her own initiative, Maria lined up a group of investors to install the first three computers. By seizing an entrepreneurial opportunity, she not only improved the amenities at her favorite hangout, but became part of a lucrative financial venture. I am excited to think of the contribution that Maria will make to Harvard's undergraduate business club.

Last year, Maria faced a devastating personal setback when her mother died after a long illness. Afterwards, she dealt with her grief in a private way, which revealed her incredible maturity and resolve. On a practical basis, Maria maintained her academic performance during this difficult time, which was not easy for her to do. She also continued her work as an artist, which allowed her to express herself creatively among her closest group of friends. As Maria's teacher, I am pleased to see her channel her grief into purposeful action; it is hard to believe that this poised and confident young woman is only seventeen.

From my perspective, Maria is a young woman with incomparable talent, strength and compassion. I am confident that she will enhance the culture at Harvard in myriad ways.

Our Assessment: This candidate is an intelligent, creative, and driven young woman who overcame the loss of her mother with grace and dignity. In this letter, her guidance counselor explains what an exceptional person she truly is.

Loss of Parents

I am delighted to write this letter of recommendation on behalf of Ms. Victoria Wyatt, who has applied for admission to Harvard University. For the past three years, Victoria has been an active member of the Women's Studies Club at Andover Academy, which I am proud to chair.

Victoria has a rich and unique character that embodies a healthy balance of old-fashioned values and twenty-first century ambition. As the only girl in a family of seven boys, Victoria has a heightened awareness of women's issues. From an early age, she has fought to participate in traditionally-male activities, such as golf and mechanics. In fact, it never occurred to Victoria that opportunities would be denied to her simply because of her gender. As a result, she proudly enrolled in Woodshop in order to cultivate her mechanical skills; Victoria also encouraged our male students to participate in our Home Economics workshops. By questioning the status quo – and encouraging others to do the same, Victoria has inspired her fellow students to follow their heart, regardless of where it will take them.

Due to a tragic series of circumstances, Victoria has had to grow up fast. After a prolonged bout with kidney disease, her mother died last year. With the help of our school counselor, Victoria moved through the ensuing adjustments with maturity and grace. She became the "woman" of the house by caring for her father and younger siblings. Victoria also helps to support the family by working a part-time job. Despite the financial and emotional pressures that have been placed on her, Victoria never uses her situation as an excuse. Instead, she has worked diligently to keep pace with her classes and graduate in the top 10% of her class.

Finally, Victoria works tirelessly to make Andover Academy a better place for her fellow students. As Class President for the past three years, she has helped to draft clear rules and regulations for student behavior on campus. Victoria has also conducted extensive research to determine the appropriate consequences for students who run afoul of school regulations. Rather than seek recognition for her efforts, Victoria prefers to work quietly and let her achievements speak for themselves. She is fully committed to using her skills to create the best environment for quality education to take place.

On a personal level, Victoria is spontaneous and genuine, with a terrific sense of humor. She will be an extraordinary addition to Harvard. Please call me if you would like to discuss her candidacy in further detail.

<u>Our Assessment</u>: By including the details about Victoria's family, this author gave the committee keen insight to her maturity, resilience and character that they could not have acquired any other way.

Candidate with a Learning Disability

Rachel Williams is a young woman with incredible artistic talent and a keen aesthetic sense. Through her relationships with her teachers, mentors and family, she has begun to carve out a career path that builds on her unusual talents and interests. I am delighted to tell you about them.

When she first enrolled at Andover Academy, Rachel had little confidence in herself. For many years, she had struggled to overcome a significant learning disability, which was not diagnosed until she was in the sixth grade. As a result, Rachel needed to find new ways to process and retrieve information. At Andover, Rachel has worked diligently to overcome this deficiency, excel in the classroom, and gain confidence in her abilities. With the support of her teachers, Rachel has discovered that she can accomplish just about everything that she sets out to do.

Rachel has a particular passion for psychology and a sincere desire to understand why people do the things they do. Analytical by nature, Rachel also has a healthy appreciation for the research behind the prevailing psychological theories. On several occasions, she asked me perceptive questions about the validity and reliability of the material that I presented in my General Psychology class. Many times, at Rachel's request, I provided illustrative examples to answer her questions and better explain the concepts. Rachel's thoughtful observations invariably brought our classroom discussions to a higher level.

Throughout the year, Rachel's engaging personality sparked many intelligent debates and brainstorming sessions. Although some of my students lacked the confidence to speak in class, Rachel aggressively engaged in the forum and showed an ongoing desire for intellectual challenge. Fortunately, she is also a good listener who picks up subtleties and ambivalence in classroom discussions. This skill, combined with Rachel's creative flair, inspired the most unique class project I have ever seen: a board game that helps players get their creative juices flowing. Rachel is convinced that everyone has creative potential that they can use to solve complex problems. The game is designed to help them find it.

Rachel came up with the idea and developed the initial prototype for the game, which other students have subsequently adapted for computer use. Inspired by its brilliance, I have demonstrated the game in several of my classes as an example of highly creative thinking. With the encouragement of her friends and faculty, Rachel is exploring the possibility of patenting the game as an educational tool. As her mentor, I feel a sense of pride in Rachel's creative success.

We are delighted to recommend Rachel Williams to your institution. She is a good and gentle young woman and a gifted student. I am certain that she will contribute great things to your campus environment.

<u>Our Assessment</u>: This author documents Rachel's learning disability without making it the primary focus on the letter. Instead, he highlights the unique strengths that she will bring to university life. The letter was well perceived.

Candidate with a Learning Disability

I am honored to support Javier Sanchez's application to Harvard. As a history teacher at Andover Academy, I taught Javier in three classes before I became his senior thesis advisor. In this capacity, I spent the better part of an academic year working closely with him on an independent research project. As a result, I feel well qualified to write this recommendation on his behalf.

From my experience, a student like Javier comes along only once or twice in a teacher's entire career. In my

58

American History class, Javier wrote an extraordinary term paper on "The History of Gender Roles in America." In the summer of 2010, I was sufficiently impressed by the paper that I approached Javier about the possibility of conducting research for me on an upcoming journal article. Afterwards, Javier did a superb job of collecting and analyzing materials for me on the evolution of the suffrage movement in America. He unearthed several unstudied documents that proved that seven legislators in rural New England were actually promoters of women's rights, despites published reports to the contrary. Inspired by these findings, Javier chose this "unreported" suffrage movement as the topic of his senior research project. I applauded his choice, both for its originality and unprecedented level of difficulty. In hindsight, I cannot remember another student being willing to tackle something even remotely as ambitious.

Javier's project was the best I have ever seen. Although he was working in a relatively unexplored area, he made convincing conjectures about the motives of the legislators and their subsequent role in the movement to promote gender equality. His paper required an enormous amount of original research and a keen ability to organize sparsely recorded data to create an accurate picture of history. Javier's writing was better than that of most college graduates I have known. Most impressively, Javier's own biases on the topic did not cloud his ability to view and report the historical record with accuracy. He was completely impartial and confronted key evidence that he wished had been different. These skills will inevitably serve him well in the future.

The only weakness in Javier's background is his disappointing SAT score, which is a reflection of his lifelong struggle with learning disabilities. Ten years ago, Javier was diagnosed with dyslexia and ADHD, which impair his ability to do well on standardized tests. Rather than request special accommodations for the exam, Javier refused to accept any special treatment. In fact, he has never requested special accommodations of any kind for any of his classes at Andover Academy. For philosophical reasons, Javier prefers not to use his affliction as justification for sub-par performance, relying instead on a rigorous set of study techniques to fuel his academic performance.

Although I wish he had scored higher on the SAT, I respect his decision to keep the focus on his talents, rather than his limitations. On the surface, his score may not seem particularly impressive, but it actually holds deep personal meaning; it proves that Javier can perform at parity with other candidates under extremely stressful circumstances. What more can you ask from a potential candidate?

Javier is not just an exceptional student, but a hardworking young man with a true zest for life. I recommend Javier without reservation for your program. If you wish to speak further about his candidacy, please feel free to contact me at (email address).

Our Assessment: In this letter, the author documents Javier's impressive skills as a writer and researcher. More importantly, he also explains why Javier refused to request special accommodations for dyslexia and ADHD, which affected his GPA and SAT scores. By presenting this material, the teacher validated Javier's essays on the same topics; he also gave his application a tangible boost.

Candidate with a Learning Disability

Dimitri Sampson is a young man with a number of exceptional talents. Because his high school record is somewhat non-traditional, his application may require a deeper review than most. I am happy to provide my impressions of this sensitive and talented young man.

Dimitri is an accomplished dancer who performs professionally with the local ballet company. At a young age, he began to spend his summers at a special camp to hone his dancing skills. While other children were playing ball and swimming at the beach, Dimitri invested many long hours in practice. As a result, he is a highly disciplined young man who continues to grow as an artist and choreographer. Every year, Dimitri and his touring troupe give a private recital to several local hospitals and retirement homes, which have cited his immense talent as a performer.

Ironically, Dimitri's depth of character originates from his early struggle to overcome his language disabilities. Although Dimitri occasionally needs extended time for assignments, he has always met or exceeded the same high academic standards as his fellow students. In fact, he is extremely reluctant to consider himself "disabled." Although eligible for extended time on the SAT, Dimitri chose to take the test as it is regularly administered, which undoubtedly lowered his scores.

Because he picks up abstract concepts with ease, Dimitri is technologically-gifted. In the past year, he has used this skill to help me create a computer database for our alumni records. Despite his lack of formal training, Dimitri is able to troubleshoot almost any computer problem. As a result, he is an invaluable resource to our staff members.

Unfortunately, a debilitating car crash in his senior year caused Dimitri to miss a great deal of course work. Although he was tutored at home, he needed to postpone his graduation by a full year. Rather than become discouraged, Dimitri resumed his studies with a renewed sense of responsibility and diligence. Since then, he has overcome numerous stumbling blocks to excel in the classroom and resume his career as a dancer. In tough times, Dimitri has continued to astound us with his optimism and determination.

If accepted to your institution, I am certain that Dimitri will find creative ways to give back to the community – he has certainly been an asset to Andover Academy. I am happy to offer him my heartfelt recommendation.

Our Assessment: This candidate endured a lot to recover from his injuries and complete his education. In this letter, his guidance counselor documents the many challenges that Dimitri faced and the graceful way that he overcame them. By doing so, she helped the committee to understand how driven and special he really is.

Chapter 14: Candidates who are Targeting a Specific School

In this chapter, we present several letters for candidates whose strengths are a perfect fit for the college or university they have chosen. To protect the privacy of the writer and applicant, the names of all people, classes, schools, places, and companies have been changed.

Great Fit for a Particular School

Ann Pierce is a remarkable student with an extraordinary talent for psychology. She demonstrated this mastery in the enclosed research paper on the "Hormonal Predictors of Schizophrenia," which she researched and wrote during the spring semester of her junior year. This fall, Ann is building on her knowledge base in the field by completing two college courses in psychology at the University of Houston. This work, in addition to her summer volunteer work as a mental health aid at Wyatt Hospital, has provided Ann with a theoretical and clinical perspective of common psychological disorders. Ultimately, her experiences have made her an excellent fit for the Clinical Psychology program at Rice University.

Since I first met Ann in 2008, she has always shown a flair for leadership and a desire to work with people. As the co-chair of the Texas Youth Advisory Panel, Ann developed an educational campaign to prevent the occurrence of eating disorders on campus, including an informative and upbeat newsletter about women's body image in contemporary society. Later, in collaboration with the Houston Health Department, she invited key speakers to the school to discuss HIV/AIDS awareness. Ann's commitment to public health education has been obvious from an early age. Her peers at Andover Academy have benefitted greatly from Ann's efforts to disseminate quality information on campus. Consequently, there is no doubt in my mind that she will take a proactive role in this regard during her four years at Rice University.

As her teacher, I have been consistently impressed by Ann's natural ability to master many different areas, which has allowed her to obtain top grades in eight AP courses. Nevertheless, I am most impressed by another of Ann's qualities: her commitment to others. As a young woman who has taken the lead in many aspects of school life – academics, research, volunteer work, and public service – Ann has repeatedly demonstrated the depth of her maturity and reliability. She is everything that a Clinical Psychologist could ever hope to be.

As an alumnus of Rice University, I am well aware of the vast educational benefits that the school will offer Ann. I am equally certain that she will be an excellent fit for the academic and clinical components of your undergraduate program in psychology. I recommend her without reservation to Rice University.

Our Assessment: Many people are asked to write recommendation letters because they are alumni of a particular college or university that the candidate is targeting. In most cases, the letter is only effective if the author knows the candidate well enough to comment on his/her fit for a particular program at the school. This is an excellent example of an alumni letter that worked. By citing Ann's research skills, volunteer work, and academic prowess, the author matched her skills to the psychology program at Rice. The letter was well perceived.

Great Fit for a Particular School

Simon Cho is a bright and tenacious student who will graduate from Andover Academy in 2012. He has an impressive command of math and science, along with a strong proclivity for solving problems. In 2010, Simon was admitted into the National Honor Society in recognition of his superior GPA. Simon's ability to excel in honors classes in science and math, in addition to his extracurricular activities, is a testament to his intelligence and organizational skills.

Fortunately, Simon also has a vibrant interest in the social sciences and world affairs, including his own heritage as a first-generation Chinese-American. In the fall of 2009, he was a student in my *Chinese 109* class, which explored diverse aspects of the Chinese culture and history. Throughout the course, Simon showed an impressive ability to integrate material from diverse sources in classroom discussions. He was particularly adept at evaluating the implications of current social issues in China, including the long-term economic effects of the "one child policy." Simon's paper on the topic revealed a level of critical thinking that I seldom observe in high school students.

As an educator, I derive tremendous satisfaction from working with students who not only master the material, but are passionate about learning; they look beyond what is presented in class and ask astute questions that stimulate lively discussions. Simon Cho is one of those students. Despite the demands of his other courses, he made a tangible contribution to my class by leading discussions on topics as diverse as international trade and old Chinese proverbs. His written assignments provided thoughtful and relevant evidence to support his conclusions; they were also well organized and efficient.

Outside the classroom, Simon is a talented athlete who holds a black belt in US. Budokai Karate. He also serves as a volunteer instructor on campus. Ironically, Simon's commitment to a healthy lifestyle was inspired by his childhood struggle with obesity. Rather than risk the possibility of serious health problems, Simon improved his fate by changing his eating habits, taking karate lessons, and transforming himself into an athlete of impeccable skill.

Throughout his years at Andover Academy, Simon has been an active member of several boxing and karate clubs, which have enabled him to provide guidance and support to other martial arts enthusiasts. By adhering to a rigid training regimen, Simon has done more than simply improve his own skills; he has set an example of selflessness and good sportsmanship for others.

Simon's diverse talents are an exceptional fit for the Asian Studies program at Stanford University, which requires the rare combination of language proficiencies and cultural sensitivity that he possesses. With Simon's vibrant intellectual curiosity and his exceptional performance in the classroom, he has much to offer your campus. I cannot imagine a better place for him to fulfill his social and academic potential.

Our Assessment: This author based his letter on the specific requirements for the Asian Studies program at Stanford. By matching Simon's accomplishments to the school's admission criteria, he yielded a focused and persuasive letter that differentiated Simon from other applicants.

Great Fit for a Particular School

I am delighted to write a letter of reference for Gretchen Smith, who I have known for the past three years. Gretchen completed three of my classes (Chemistry I & II and Analytical Chemistry) and achieved "A" grades in each. She also distinguished herself as a highly motivated and talented scientist. Most of our students are challenged to complete our traditional science program and wouldn't dream of attempting honors courses. Gretchen willingly accepted the opportunity. In her junior and senior years, she juggled the demands of six AP courses, in addition to completing an independent research project. To date, she has completed two studies on the effects of reduced salt intake on weight loss in teenage girls. Throughout her coursework and independent research, Gretchen was always organized, cheerful and willing to help others. She demonstrated excellent potential for a career in the sciences.

Gretchen's research success was partially attributable to her strong interpersonal skills. She works well with all types of people and quickly puts others at ease. A huge challenge in her research was explaining the diet and exercise protocol to the participating children and their families. Gretchen quickly established a positive rapport with all 50 subjects and their parents. She patiently answered their questions and encouraged the children who were ambivalent about participating. Long after the completion of the study, Gretchen continued to keep in touch with several families to offer encouraging tips to promote further weight loss. I am certain that the project would not have been successful without her graciousness and dedication.

I am also impressed by Gretchen's initiative outside the classroom. During her sophomore year, she started a small internet/mail order business selling hand-painted T-shirts. She researched the field on her own and did all of the web design work herself. At first, I was surprised that Gretchen took on such a venture, but she thrived under the bustling schedule. Her shirts were extremely popular on campus; I often saw her selling them from a small booth she set up outside our student union. I initially chuckled at Gretchen's creative way to earn a few dollars on the side. I later discovered that the business netted almost $20,000 during its first year, which covered the costs of her summer program at Oxford University.

I had to marvel at Gretchen's initiative, organizational skills and willingness to take risks. During the past year, she also became an employer, as she expanded her business to the local state university. In this capacity, she has already developed many practical skills in marketing, manufacturing, web site design, advertising, payroll and time management. I am certain that this success is only the first of many for Gretchen.

When selecting a college, Gretchen questioned whether she should pursue a program in the sciences or business. She ultimately chose the University of Pennsylvania because the school offers a dual program in both areas at the undergraduate level. It is the perfect place for someone like Gretchen, who has the interest and talent to excel in both fields. The future offers many exciting opportunities for scientists who possess the skills to commercialize their own technologies. I offer Gretchen my highest recommendation. With her strong intellect and exuberant entrepreneurial spirit, there are no limits to what this tenacious woman will achieve.

Our Assessment: This author is a noted teacher at a private prep school who rarely writes such strong letters of support. Her detailed explanation of Gretchen's strengths in science and business, including her impressive entrepreneurial success, made a positive impression on the committee.

Great Fit for a Particular School

I am pleased to write this letter of recommendation on behalf of Lorelai Stevens, who was a student in two of my literature classes at Andover Academy. I also supervised her community service project. Through our affiliation, I have watched Lorelai grow into a poised and accomplished young woman with excellent work habits and superior interpersonal skills. She is one of my favorite students.

For her senior project, Lorelai developed and managed an investment club at a local retirement community. Lorelai's job was to recruit the participants and explain the risk/reward profile of various investment options. Throughout the semester, Lorelai did an exceptional job of explaining the different stock sectors to 36 novice investors. She patiently answered questions, discussed brokerage house options, and taught the participants how to research their picks on the Internet. The group not only made money; they had great fun. Throughout the semester, I watched Lorelai become more confident in her ability to manage a challenging project. The investment club was an unqualified success, largely because of her dedication.

In addition to her academic success in the Honors curriculum at Andover, Lorelai is also a talented vocalist with strong ties to community theatre. In 2010, while performing in "Don Giovanni," Lorelai became fascinated by the short story upon which the opera was based. We enjoyed several after-class discussions about the work, whose meaning is often debated by seasoned literary critics. Lorelai became intrigued by the work's subtleties, noting that its interpretation depended upon the language in which it was read; the French to English translation of specific words created considerable ambiguity. After reading the French version of the story, Lorelai wrote a superb analysis of the compromises inherent in the English translation. Her paper, which was flawless, remains a crown jewel in the English department.

Lorelai is a motivated young woman of numerous talents and considerable self-discipline. Whether studying derivative curves, writing an essay, or preparing for an operatic performance, she gives each endeavor her full focus and attention. This passion and determination are rare and precious gifts.

In my 25 years of teaching, I have known few other students with Lorelai's talent and drive. I am certain that she will be an asset to Harvard, which offers exceptional programs in literature and the arts. As a graduate of the same programs at Harvard (MS, 1976, PhD, 1980), I am excited to think of the unique contribution that Lorelai will make.

Our Assessment: The strength of this letter is that the author knows the applicant well and is favorably impressed by her work. The writer did a great job of citing specific examples of Lorelai's financial expertise and community service work. She also documented the candidate's unusual skills as a vocalist and writer. By citing Lorelai's tenacity and discipline, she distinguished her from hundreds of other applicants with similar academic achievements.

Chapter 15: Candidates with Room to Grow

Many times, candidates do not peak until well after high school, when they discover their interests and begin to fulfill their highest potential. In these situations, a thoughtful letter that documents their strengths, explains their blemishes, and offers the support of a teacher or guidance counselor can have a positive impact on the admissions decision.

In this chapter, we present several letters that were written on behalf of students who have room to grow. To protect the privacy of the writer and applicant, the names of all people, classes, schools, places, and companies have been changed.

Candidate with Room to Grow

Steven Medeiros has been a student at the Andover Academy since the ninth grade. Unfortunately, a death in his family during his sophomore year prevented him from putting his education first. After recovering from this loss, Steven has regained his enthusiasm for school and is living up to his original potential.

With a renewed interest in mathematics, Steven has chosen to take a college course in calculus at Kaiser College. Although the commute is lengthy and the material is difficult for him, Steven is happy to embrace this challenge. Knowing his interest in an engineering career, I applaud his efforts to distinguish himself in this area.

When not involved in his studies, Steven is the night manager at his father's Jiffy Lube franchise, where he changes oil and diagnoses minor mechanical problems. Steven has matured greatly from this work experience, which has taught him how to build relationships with his customers and co-workers. Steven has also has launched an entrepreneurial project this semester by offering duct cleaning services to residential clients in the tri-county area. To balance the demands of a fledgling business with his heavy course load, Steven has developed a workable schedule that will allow ample time for studying commuting, and various contingencies. While helping him to develop it, I was impressed by Steven's logical approach and determination to succeed. He has matured significantly in the past few years.

Although Steven was initially reticent to join extracurricular activities, he has recently joined the school softball team. I view this step as a positive example of his commitment to personal growth.

Steven's combination of intellectual curiosity and emotional growth suggest that he is ready for the challenges that college will present. If admitted, I believe he will be a positive influence at your school. Please call me if you would like to discuss his candidacy in additional detail.

Our Assessment: During his sophomore year of high school, Steven's mother was killed in a car accident, which devastated his entire family. Afterwards, he struggled to succeed in school and find his niche at Andover Academy. In this letter, his guidance counselor offers supportive words about his progress, without discussing the situation in detail (which was Steven's preference). The letter was well perceived.

Candidate with Room to Grow

Laurel Stoddard is a young woman with a great enthusiasm for learning and a strong determination to meet the challenges that life presents. Last year, when she discovered that she was pregnant, Laurel decided to accelerate her academic program in order to graduate a year early. Although our school administrators advised her against this, she was determined to fulfill her graduation requirements.

By embarking on an ambitious study program, Laurel accepted the challenge with gusto and completed all of her work on time. On several occasions, when her interest was aroused, Laurel completed extra credit projects that went above and beyond what was required of her. By doing so, she earned a perfect GPA and the respect of all of her teachers.

Because of financial problems at home, along with the complications of raising a newborn, Laurel must work long hours in order to support her family. From all reports, she is an excellent employee with a solid work ethic. Over time, Laurel has learned how to use her strong native intelligence to solve problems, overcome obstacles, and achieve her goals. Although she is just sixteen years old, Laurel is an accomplished young woman with an uncommon level of maturity. She has much to offer whatever college she chooses to attend.

<u>Our Assessment</u>: This candidate made the difficult choice to have her baby, raise it alone, and complete high school a year early in order to support her family. In this short but persuasive letter, her guidance counselor explains those circumstances to the admissions committee. Ironically, this letter's greatest strength is that the writer does not judge Laurel in any way – or make any comments that go beyond her role as a guidance counselor. Instead, she limits her comments to factual statements that explain the situation and support Laurel's goals.

Candidate with Room to Grow

Philip O'Brian is exceptionally bright and witty. Unlike his peers, who tend to shy away from math and logic, Philip is "at home" in these complex disciplines, which require a flair for abstract thought. He is a well-liked member of our school community, who brings a refreshing perspective to all of his endeavors.

An avid reader, Philip has a natural desire to understand the world through history, music and literature. The son of a commercial airline pilot, Philip is also the only student at Andover Academy who can fly an airplane. Getting his pilot's license was a critical goal for Philip, which inspired him to master the relevant material in math and science. He has also completed dual enrollment classes in logic and C++ at a local college, which allowed him to launch a start-up company developing web sites for aspiring pilots.

At school, Philip works to capacity, but he occasionally doubts his abilities. He has also wrestled with a persistent case of shyness that prevents him from participating in most outside activities. Thankfully, as he comes closer to achieving his goal of flying, his confidence has started to soar. The improvements in his grade point average have been quite promising.

It is a joy to see Philip apply to college with a newfound sense of confidence. The aeronautics program at your institution will provide an excellent match for his abilities and interests. I am happy to recommend him.

<u>Our Assessment</u>: Every school has a student like Philip, who is brilliant, creative, and painfully shy. In this letter, the author presents his shyness as growing pains, rather than a character flaw. By selling Philip's strengths, including his passion for flying, he also explained the boy's natural fit for a program in aeronautics. The letter was well perceived.

Chapter 16: Hall of Shame: References That Do NOT Open Doors

Throughout this book, we have offered numerous examples of terrific recommendation letters. From an admissions perspective, our discussion would not be complete unless we included a few samples of bad letters that failed to enhance the candidates' applications. Sad to say, but the letters in this chapter are typical of what we see for many college applicants. How do they wind up with such lackluster references? Three possibilities come to mind:

1. The author did not know what to say, so (s)he said as little as possible.

2. The author was not particularly enthusiastic about the candidate, but did not decline his/her request for a letter.

3. The author blatantly sabotaged the candidate, for any number of reasons.

By publishing these bad letters, we hope to demonstrate the difference between a great reference letter and a mediocre one. In the admissions game, it can make the difference between acceptance and rejection.

For applicants, this chapter is compelling evidence of why you should choose your writers carefully and give them as much supporting documentation as possible. For writers, these letters are a convenient yardstick for you to use when you are asked to write a letter of recommendation. As a general rule, if you cannot be any more enthusiastic about a candidate than the authors of the letters in this chapter, you should decline the applicant's request for a letter. You are NOT helping the candidate if you are ambiguous, ambivalent, or unwilling to provide sufficient details.

Ambivalent Letter

Melanie Riggs is a bright and energetic young woman who has assumed numerous leadership positions at Andover Academy. Thus far, I have been her professor in three English classes, in which Melanie received "B" grades.

Compared to her peers in the department, Melanie is an above-average student. At times, she gives 100% to her studies and amazes us with her performance. Other times, Melanie becomes overwhelmed and does not live up to her true potential. From my perspective, this may be due to maturity issues; in every respect, Melanie seems to be a late bloomer.

Despite her motivational issues, Melanie has managed to accelerate academically by taking senior level classes during her junior year. This fall, Melanie has enrolled in an AP course in Chemistry, which requires substantial lab time and a significant amount of outside preparation. Thankfully, Melanie has been able to handle this new challenge in addition to her other academic commitments.

This past year, Melanie's impressive participation in the Business Club has confirmed her leadership potential. We believe that she is "stepping up to the plate" for the next chapter in her life, and once established in college, she will be able to reveal the gifts that we know she possesses. We are happy to recommend her to your institution.

Our Assessment: Although filled with compliments, this letter sabotaged Melanie's chance to get into a top tier school. The second paragraph, which describes her as "a late bloomer" and "not living up to her true potential," told the committee that Melanie was NOT a serious student. Even worse is the author's frequent use of the term "we," which implies that she is speaking not just for herself, but for her entire department. College is a serious endeavor; it should not be the first time that a candidate "steps to the plate" and fulfills his/her potential. Sadly, this type of ambivalence in an academic reference letter will tank even the strongest application.

Nothing but the Facts

Samantha Jones worked for me as an Accounting Clerk at the Hilton Hotel from December of 2009 to August of 2012. During that time, she was promoted once and received two annual raises. Her performance reviews were "Above Average" and noted her efficiency and organizational skills. All of her assignments, including our annual tax return, were completed on time and within expectations.

Samantha left the Hilton Hotel to accept a position as a Junior Accountant at the Ramada Inn in Cambridge. We were sorry to see her go. We wish Samantha all the best in the future.

<u>Our Assessment</u>: This letters includes positive information, but not nearly enough to make an admissions decision. By failing to discuss Samantha's strengths, or relate them to the requirements of a particular college, the author gave the reader no reason to be enthusiastic about her. In fact, by providing such a terse letter, the author made the committee wonder what she WASN'T saying.

Mild Sabotage

It is a pleasure to recommend Michael Hightower to Harvard University. An active young man with a love of the outdoors, Michael has a highly adventurous spirit. Consequently, he is excited about the prospect of enrolling in your school's unique curriculum in Environmental Management.

Michael has attended Andover Academy since his sophomore year. Over the past three years, he has developed a strong personality and a deep sense of purpose. At 14, Michael was diagnosed with a learning disability that required a customized approach to studying. He transferred to Andover after his freshman year, when the public high school he attended did not provide the level of support that he desired. Michael has done much better on our close-knit campus. Although he was often frustrated, he worked hard to master subject areas that were incredibly difficult for him. Thanks to the tireless support of his advisor, Dr. Wong, Michael was able to find his place on campus.

By completing high school one semester early, Michael has cleared his schedule to participate in a one-semester program at the University of Alaska, where he will research the dioxin levels in swordfish. The data he is gathering will be used to support a university research project on environmental safety in rural food supplies. The skills that Michael is developing in data collection and management will be well-utilized in his college program in Environmental Management.

I support Michael's decision to participate in such a challenging venture, considering his previous problems adjusting to new situations. Thankfully, the program in Alaska is well-organized and well-supervised. By the time Michael gets to Harvard, he will already have several critical skills under his belt, including the ability to thrive in a large, unknown environment.

By pursuing the program in Alaska, Michael has shown us that he knows how to set a goal and see it through. Hopefully, he will succeed. I wish Michael the best in his pursuit of an excellent education.

<u>Our Assessment</u>: This letter appears to have been written by two different people: one who supports Michael, and another who thinks he is immature and incapable of handling adult responsibilities. By mentioning his problems adapting to life situations, the author negated all of the great things he said about Michael's work in Alaska. He repeatedly called attention to a negative, rather than cite the candidate's strengths. As a result, the reader walks away confused about how strongly the author is endorsing Michael.

Summary

After reading this book, including 45 successful reference letters, we hope that you feel well-prepared to write (or obtain) a persuasive recommendation letter for college.

A Quick Summary for Candidates:

1. Ask people who know you well enough to highlight your strengths (and are willing to do so).

2. Give each author enough information to do a good job for you, including:

   a. a cover letter with the names, addresses and deadlines for all of the letters you need   (Appendix 2)
   b. the appropriate forms from each school that the writer needs to complete
   c. a summary of your "Match Points" (Appendix 3)
   d. a current copy of your resume
   e. your application essays
   f. pre-addressed, stamped envelopes for all letters

3. Give the author enough time to write a compelling letter.

4. Follow through with each author to ensure that his/her letter reaches its destination.

5. Thank the author for his/her efforts on your behalf.

A Quick Summary for Letter Writers:

1. Meet with the candidate to determine whether you are the best person to write a reference letter on his/her behalf.

2. If you agree to write a letter, give the candidate a copy of the Reference Letter Request Form (Appendix 5), which summarizes all of the information you will need.

3. Do not begin until you have all of the requested documents.

4. Review your organization's policy regarding letters of recommendation. Limit your comments to positive, factual observations that you have actually observed in your interactions with the applicant.

5. Follow our guidelines in Chapter 5 to write the best letter possible.

6. For additional help in writing and editing letters of recommendation, admissions essays, and personal statements, please visit www.ivyleagueadmission.com.

In the college admissions process, reference letters can provide the committee with objective, third-party documentation of a candidate's strengths and skills. A well-crafted reference letter can also explain a variety of personal circumstances (and obstacles) better than any essay ever could. By harnessing the power of your recommendations, you will improve your chances of gaining admission to the top universities in the country. Don't miss this chance to claim your destiny!

Appendices

Appendix 1:   Sample Rating Sheet

<u>Factors</u>:   For each factor below, please indicate your opinion of this applicant's rating on that factor relative to other candidates you have observed.

Ranking Standards:

1. Exceptional, top 5%
2. Excellent, next 10%
3. Good, next 20%
4. Average, middle 30%
5. Reservation, next 30%
6. Poor, low 5%
7. No basis for judgment

Factors:

_____ **Emotional Stability:**   Exhibits stable moods; performs under pressure

_____ **Interpersonal Relations:**   Rapport with others; cooperation, attitude toward supervisors

_____ **Judgment:**   Ability to analyze problems, common sense; decisiveness

_____ **Resourcefulness:**   Originality; initiative, management of resources and time

_____ **Reliability:**   Dependability; sense of responsibility, promptness; conscientiousness

_____ **Perseverance:**   Stamina; endurance, psychological strength

_____ **Communication skills:**   Clarity in writing and speech

_____ **Self-confidence:** Assuredness; awareness of strengths & weaknesses

_____ **Empathy:**   Consideration; tact; sensitivity to the needs of others

_____ **Maturity:**   Personal development; social awareness, ability to cope with life situations

_____ **Intellectual curiosity:**   Desire to learn and extend beyond expectations

_____ **Scholarship:** Ability to learn, quality of study habits, native intellectual ability

_____ **Motivation:**   Depth of commitment; intensity; sincerity of career choice

Evaluation Summary:

Compared to other applicants you know, please provide an overall evaluation of this candidate:

( ) Exceptional candidate, top 5%
( ) Excellent candidate, next 10%
( ) Good candidate, next 20%
( ) Average candidate, middle 30%
( ) Weak candidate, bottom 35%
( ) No basis for judgment

Appendix 2:   Request for Reference Letters

Name:
Date:
Address:
Phone:
Email:

Dr./Mr./Mrs./Ms.   _____,

I appreciate your willingness to write me a strong letter of recommendation for college. This page summarizes the schools to which I am applying and the name(s) and address(es) of each person to whom the letter(s) should be addressed. For your convenience, I have listed the schools in the order in which the letters need to be received (the earliest deadlines are listed first).

I am enclosing several pages of supporting information:

a) A list of my Match Points, which explain how my credentials match the school's requirements
c) A current copy of my resume
d) My application essays
e) Pre-addressed, stamped envelopes for all letters

Please let me know if you need additional information.   Thank you for your support.

1) School 1:   Name and Address of School
                 Name of Contact Person to Whom Letter Should be Addressed
                 Date Letter Should be Mailed to School
                 Additional Information / Instructions (if any)

2) School 2:   Name and Address of School
                 Name of Contact Person to Whom Letter Should be Addressed
                 Date Letter Should be Mailed to School
                 Additional Information / Instructions (if any)

3) School 3:   Name and Address of School
                 Name of Contact Person to Whom Letter Should be Addressed
                 Date Letter Should be Mailed to School
                 Additional Information / Instructions (if any)

If you have any questions or concerns, please contact me at the phone number and email address above. Thank you again for your support.

71

Appendix 3: Bethany Daniel's Preparation for College (Match Points)

My Preparation:

1. **Academic Preparation.** My academic background is an excellent match for Harvard. I will graduate from Andover Academy with a 4.0 GPA, including perfect grades in five AP courses.

2. **Professional Experience.** I have worked part-time as a receptionist in a medical office for the past two years. Additionally, I have tutored several students in math and science, which has taught me how communicate scientific concepts in an understandable way.

3. **Communication skills:** excellent speaker and writer; member of the Andover debate team, which won third place in the national competition in 2012.

4. **Outside Interests.** I am a tri-athlete who competes at the state, local and national levels. I am also a volunteer paramedic for the local ambulance company.

5. **Empathy:** high emotional intelligence; assumed workload for a fellow debater after a debilitating car accident. Visited the student often during her medical leave and provided a consistent source of emotional support.

6. **Language Skills:** fluent in English, Spanish and Chinese; frequently translate documents and journal articles for faculty members.

7. **Motivation:** completed a research project about fraternal twins for my psychology class; received an A grade.

With my excellent academic background, strong interpersonal skills, and commitment to helping others, I am a great fit for the pre-medical curriculum at Harvard; I also possess the maturity to pursue my education with purpose and enthusiasm.

Thoughts for my Recommendation Letter:

As my math teacher, you taught three of my courses (Algebra I & II, Trigonometry), in which I earned A grades. As a result, you observed the following strengths:

1. **Intellectual Drive:** I have consistently taken the most difficult courses and excelled in them. I have also contributed to class discussions and tackled the hardest problems in the homework set, which required strong analytical and quantitative skills

2. **Teaching Skills:** I tutored three students in Algebra I, which allowed them to improve their grade from a D to a B within six weeks. I also improved my communication skills

3. **Discipline:** I balanced my classes with a part-time job and participation in several outside activities

4. **Empathy & Motivation:** I work well with people from different racial and socioeconomic backgrounds. I have also assumed leadership roles in several groups, to increase my contribution to them.

Appendix 4:   Sample Thank You Note for a Reference Letter

October 1, 2012

Lawrence Johnson, Esq.
Abbott Laboratories
333 Island Drive
Warren, CT   02876

Dear Mr. Johnson,

Thank you for taking the time to write a recommendation letter to support my application to Harvard. I appreciate the timeliness of your reply and the gracious compliments in your letter.

By working in your laboratory during my summer breaks, I had a wonderful chance to work with several Harvard alumni, who convinced me that it was the perfect place for me to complete my undergraduate education. My first-hand experience with you and your staff was instrumental in my decision to pursue a career in medical research. Thank you for giving me the opportunity to work on such significant projects at an early stage of my career. Without your guidance and support, I would not have the confidence to pursue such an ambitious goal.

I will contact you during the admissions process to apprise you of my progress. Thank you again for the reference letter and for your kindness to me over the years. You've been an exceptional mentor and role model.

Sincerely,

Erica Page

Appendix 5: Reference Letter Request Form

Thank you for inquiring about the possibility of obtaining a reference letter from me. Please follow these steps to ensure that I can do a great job on your behalf.

Step 1: Arrange an Initial Meeting to Discuss the Letter

Please schedule a meeting with me to talk about the recommendation letter **at least four weeks before** you need it. Ask me if I would feel comfortable writing a supportive and positive recommendation for you.

When asked to provide a reference, I have to ask myself if I know you well enough to support your application for a particular college. Acknowledging the importance of a top-quality endorsement, I would rather decline the request to write a reference than write a vague or mediocre one. Let's meet face-to-face to discuss whether or not I am the right person to write your letter.

Step 2: Provide All Relevant Documentation

If we agree that I should write your letter during our face-to-face meeting, please be prepared to provide the following documents:

a. A cover sheet with the names, addresses and deadlines for all of the letters you need
b. The appropriate forms from each school that I will need to complete
c. A ONE-page summary of the accomplishments you want me to mention
d. A current copy of your resume (including your awards, publications and honors)
e. Your application essays
f. Pre-addressed, stamped envelopes for all letters.
g. Also feel free to include ONE page of additional information that you feel will help me write the letter. This may include specific anecdotes and stories you want me to mention, along with additional details about projects or papers I have seen that would demonstrate your creativity, intelligence, writing abilities or technical skills. Please type all information. You should waive your right to read the letter of recommendation, keeping in mind that I will still give you a copy for your records.

Note: I will NOT write the letter unless I have all of the documents listed above.

Step 3: Follow-up

Once I receive the documents, I will confirm an exact date that your letter will be sent. One week after the expected date of arrival, please verify that the letter has reached its destination. If the college has NOT received the letter within 10 days, please let me know. I will send another copy.

Thank you for adhering to these guidelines.

Professor John Smith, 111 Rogers Hall, (555)-555-5555, jsmith@andover.edu

Made in the USA
Lexington, KY
28 October 2014